Rebels in Eden

Mass Politica

by

Little

Rebels in Eden

Violence in the United States

Richard E. Rubenstein

Brown and Company   Boston · Toronto

LIBRARY OF CONGRESS CATALOG CARD NO. 73-99898

FIRST EDITION

Published simultaneously in Canada
by Little, Brown & Company (Canada) Limited

PRINTED IN THE UNITED STATES OF AMERICA

To Libby

If ever the free institutions of America are destroyed, that event may be attributed to the omnipotence of the majority, which may at some future time urge the minorities to desperation and oblige them to have recourse to physical force. Anarchy will then be the result, but it will have been brought about by despotism.

— ALEXIS DE TOQUEVILLE
Democracy in America

Decolonization is always a violent phenomenon.

— FRANTZ FANON
The Wretched of the Earth

Prefatory Note

Some, reading this work, may feel that it is intended to justify the resort to force by blacks or other domestic groups. Others may criticize it for failing to underwrite particular revolts. On the contrary, its aim is neither to condone nor to condemn, but to understand why, in a constitutional democracy, so much violence has accompanied the rise of so many groups to power.

Easy moral judgments are a dime a dozen these days. Still they are too expensive. With the future of America's cities hanging in the balance, one's initial approval or disapproval of violent uprisings or confrontations becomes irrelevant. Hiding behind a façade of moralism it is all too easy to prescribe shallow solutions to problems of civil disorder, and then to attribute failure to the incorrigibility of the violent rather than to one's own superficiality. The platitudes of well-intentioned reformers are surely as dangerous, in this respect, as the "shoot to kill" responses of authoritarians. Superficiality has now become not merely an academic sin but a potential *casus belli.*

This disclaimer of any intention to moralize does not, of course, imply that the work which follows is free of value judgments. On the contrary, it would not have been written but for an intuition, no doubt inspired by sympathy, that the apparently aberrant and lawless acts of certain domestic groups were in some way generated by the normal operation of the political system. The facts, however, compelled an advance beyond simple moralizing; it was necessary to attempt to understand and explain not merely the violent revolts of one's friends, but those of one's enemies (for example, nativists and racists).

Out of this attempt there emerged, finally, a perspective on America which I had not previously imagined, in which violence itself seemed a good deal less important than the group relationships which produced it. The reader may or may not come to share this perspective. Hopefully, no matter what his views, he will be emboldened to renew his own search for a "usable past."

RICHARD E. RUBENSTEIN

Chicago, Illinois
September 15, 1969

Acknowledgments

The Adlai Stevenson Institute in Chicago, Illinois, made it possible for me to write this book by appointing me a fellow of the institute in 1967 and assistant director in 1968. I am grateful to William R. Polk, director, and to the fellows and staff of the institute for their counsel and friendship.

By virtue of affiliation with this organization, I had the opportunity to participate in the regular meetings of a special study group on violent politics and social change led by Manfred Halpern of Princeton University and Wayne Fredericks of the Ford Foundation. In addition, I was able to discuss the ideas presented here with the faculty members and students of numerous colleges and universities associated with the institute. To all those now striving to relate the phenomena of political violence to the complexities of social change, my admiration and thanks.

Special acknowledgments are owed, of course, to those

friends who have read and criticized portions of the manuscript: William Kornhauser of the University of California at Berkeley, Charles V. Hamilton of Columbia University, Edward W. Gude of Dartmouth College, Jerome H. Skolnick of the University of California at San Diego, Richard M. Pfeffer of Johns Hopkins University, Richard M. Curtis of New York City, Milton Viorst of Washington, D.C., and Joseph Muskrat, Eqbal Ahmad and Thomas J. Boodell, Jr. of the Stevenson Institute. Charles B. Everitt of Little, Brown and Company was both patient editor and helpful critic. Thanks, too, are due Ruth Muller, who helped prepare the manuscript for publication. She has reminded me to state that the views expressed here are not necessarily those of the aforementioned readers or of the Adlai Stevenson Institute.

The book is dedicated to my wife, without whose loving support I would not have had the strength to change careers, cities or perspectives.

R.E.R.

Contents

Contents

Rebels in Eden

The Myth of

The assassination of President John F. Kennedy marked a major turning point in American history. In the year following the President's death, America seemed to turn a corner, to enter into a new phase of national existence, a strange new world in which the concerns of 1963 seemed as antiquated as those of 1933.

The pace of change accelerated drastically. History seemed to run forward like a motion picture with the projector out of control. Before one's eyes weird metamorphoses took place: an insignificant little war in Southeast Asia became a gigantic national enterprise; peaceable Negroes marching on Washington became hostile mobs, burning and looting in virtually every major city; college students headed for the Peace Corps (one's own children!) became revolutionaries or hippies. Especially for those who came to maturity prior to the 1960's, entering this new world was a profoundly disturbing experience. It was

2

1.

Peaceful Progress

the sort of nightmare in which everything is familiar, yet unfamiliar, superficially stable, yet shifting underfoot like quicksand. A political coalition which had lasted thirty years was breaking up. The nation's enemies abroad were no longer clearly identifiable, and neither were her allies. Standards of sexual behavior, social worth and artistic integrity were all in motion. Most disturbing of all, the new age reeked of violence, for in addition to war and private crime (which had been present continuously) acts of political violence — riots, assassinations, ghetto "shoot-outs" and confrontations between police and demonstrators — were becoming commonplace.

If after November 22, 1963, the nation went into shock, subsequent events from Watts to the assassination of Senator Robert Kennedy and the 1968 National Democratic convention in Chicago ensured that the traumatized state would endure. One result, not surprisingly, was a kind of mental anesthesia — a refusal to come to terms with the problem of political violence and its relationship to the American experience. It was not until the death of the second Kennedy in June 1968 that President Johnson appointed a commission to study the problem; and even then, the commission's most honest academic experts were compelled to admit that they knew very little about the causes, nature and consequences of domestic political violence — that, in fact, their studies were just beginning. The intellectuals, in other words, shared the common anesthesia. Like everyone else they sought refuge from the pain of the present in comforting myths about the past.

Thus, more than five years of assassinations, ghetto uprisings, student revolts, tumultuous demonstrations and violent police action have produced no systematic reevaluation of the role of political violence in American history. Notwithstanding a mountain of written words on "the urban crisis," "the racial question" and similar contemporary topics, many scholars continue to write as if domestic political violence were a creation of the 1960's, and the past had nothing to say to the present. It seems, as Clifford Geertz has said, that "we do not want to learn too much about ourselves too quickly."

The fact is that the present state of domestic disorder in the United States is not the product of some destructive quality mysteriously ingrained in the substance of American life. It is a product of a long sequence of particular events whose interconnections our received categories of self-understanding are not only inadequate to reveal but are designed to conceal. We do not know very well what kind of society we live in, what kind of history we have had, what kind of people we are. We are just now beginning to find out, the hard way . . . [1]

Ironically, as Geertz suggests, despite the fact that we are a nation of amateur historians, we do not know "what kind of history we have had." But this is not surprising. Societies troubled by internal conflict and moral doubt often explore the past more for justification than enlightenment.

The Puritans of New England, uneasy about the conversion of their God-centered "city on a hill" into an acquisitive, profit-dominated society, produced the first American histories: "vindications" of God's plan for America. The greatest historian of the pre–Civil War period, George Bancroft, was a Democratic politician chiefly interested in justifying America's right to expand territorially. In the age of industrial expansion both American history and the nascent social sciences celebrated the rise of big business to preeminence. Even the bolder Progressive scholars of the present century wrote American history as a success story, with working-class democracy and "people's capitalism" in the starring roles. Small wonder, then, that during the 1950's and early 1960's a nation seeking domestic unity and world hegemony should turn for reassurance to the modern historians, political philosophers and social scientists of the "consensus" school.

The United States, consensus scholars believed, was the one nation in which extremely diverse groups had learned to compromise their differences peaceably. American society, they held, was blessed by a blurring of divisions between a multiplicity of economic, social, political and ethnic groups. For one reason or another (either because the land was fertile or the people hardworking, or because no true aristocracy or proletariat ever developed on American soil, or because the two-party system worked so well) any sizable domestic group could gain its proper share of power, prosperity and respectability merely by playing the game according to the rules. In the process, the group itself would tend to lose coherence and to be incorporated into the great middle class. The result, it was said, was something unique in world history — real progress without violent group conflict. In such an America there was no need — there never had been a need — for political violence. Rising domestic groups had not been compelled to be revolutionary, nor had the "ins" generally resorted to force to keep them out. America had mastered the art of peaceful power transference, a feat which established both her uniqueness as a nation and her fitness to lead the world.

This is the myth of peaceful progress, which since the racial uprisings beginning in 1964 has spawned a corollary — the myth of Negro uniqueness. For clearly, the only way to explain what happened in Watts, Newark and Detroit without challenging the prevailing belief in the norm of peaceful progress is to assume that black people are historically aberrant — the exception to the rule. Adherence to the myth cuts across party lines, with conservatives emphasizing black laziness, loose morality and disrespect for law, and liberals discussing the weakness of Negro family structure, the prevalence of racial discrimination and the culture of poverty. Either way, it is assumed that the existing political and economic system can make good on its promise to blacks without radical institutional change. The situation can be salvaged, faith in America confirmed, and violence ended without any great national political upheaval, so long as the government spends enough money on both reform programs and law enforcement.

"This then is the mood of America's absolutism," wrote Louis Hartz, "the sober faith that its norms are self-evident." [2] But what if the black community is not unique at all, but merely the latest of a long line of domestic groups motivated to resort to violence? What if the institutions designed to make economic and political advancement possible have broken down frequently in the past, compelling other large groups to embrace the politics of violence? What if political violence on a massive scale is, as H. Rap Brown has stated, "as American as cherry pie"? Then, clearly, the myth of peaceful progress collapses and the immunity of hallowed domestic institutions from criticism is at an end.

Particularly if prior outbreaks of violent revolt in America are found to be patterned, the suspicion may arise that not just violence-prone or "exceptional" groups are responsible, but American institutions themselves — or at least the relationship between certain groups and certain institutions. In such event, modern Americans may be compelled to stop worrying exclusively about black skin and white prejudice, and start wondering whether something more fundamental is wrong — something not merely psychological and temporary, but structural and (so far) permanent. That this has not happened testifies not only to the severity of the trauma but to the remarkable staying power of the myth of peaceful progress. Indeed, the myth continues even now to shape our attitudes towards political violence.

Whether in the White House, Congress or the street, reactions to recent riots and demonstrations reveal a widely held belief that such episodes are "un-American"— rare occurrences in American life bearing little relationship to the way other domestic groups succeeded in advancing themselves. As we shall see, this is a false assumption. For more than two hundred years, from the Indian wars and farmer uprisings of the eighteenth century to the labor-management and racial disturbances of the twentieth, the United States has experienced regular episodes of serious mass violence related to the social, political and economic objectives of insurgent groups. Nevertheless, the

7

shocked question "How can this be happening here?" implies that mass violence in America is anomalous. More important, the question implies its own answer: mass violence is the product of group characteristics (disrespect for law, mob hysteria, or sheer impatience) rather than characteristics of the social system (elitism, exclusion of political minorities or economic exploitation). In order to preserve intact the myth of peaceful progress we generate a steady stream of racist stereotypes (the "Indian savage," "wild Irishman" or "unassimilable Negro") which are intended to explain group violence without implicating the existing social or political system. In other words, the assumption that *violence* is un-American forces the conclusion that *the violent* are un-American — alien, racially inferior perhaps, or under foreign domination. The result of such reasoning, as will be seen, has sometimes been to involve Americans in suppression of minorities on a genocidal scale.

Closely associated with the belief in the abnormality of domestic political violence is the idea that riots or insurrections in the United States have always been both unnecessary and useless. Given the assumption of the adequacy of existing institutions to advance the interests of oppressed minorities, how could one reason otherwise? The proposition, however, is fallacious no matter how one interprets it. For example, it is false if it means that the established political machinery has permitted all major "out-groups" to move nonviolently up the ladder of power. On the contrary, our individualistic institutions seem better designed to facilitate the advancement of talented individuals than oppressed groups. Most groups which have engaged in mass violence have done so only after a long period of fruitless, relatively nonviolent struggle in which established procedures have been tried and found wanting.

Similarly, the proposition is false if it means that the established order is self-transforming, or that groups in positions of power will always share that power with outsiders without being threatened by actual or potential violence. The eighteenth-century farmer revolts, as well as tumultuous urban demonstrations in sympathy with the French Revolution, were used by Jeffersonians to create a new two-party system over the horrified protests of the Federalists. Northern violence ended the southern slave kingdom and southern terrorism ended Radical Reconstruction. The transformation of labor-management relations was achieved during a wave of bloody strikes in the midst of a depression and amid widespread fear of revolution. And black people in urban ghettos made their greatest political gains, both in Congress and in the cities, during the racial strife of the 1960's.

We may assert, therefore, that domestic political violence is neither un-American nor, in every case, unnecessary and useless. To this we must add: outbreaks of mass violence in America are not always, or even usually, the products of outside agitation, incitement to riot, foreign influence or conspiracy by a small minority. Although those engaging in violent action are almost always a minority of any given group (just as the United States Army constitutes a minority of American citizens), most major uprisings have expressed the felt desires and perceived interests of large domestic groups. Of course, it is traditional for those in power to deny that mass violence is representative, for to admit this would be to confess that the political system is failing. Thus, the ghetto uprisings of the 1960's were attributed to a few "mean and willful men" (President Johnson after the Detroit riot of 1967), the lawless and the unemployed (California Governor's Commission reporting on the Watts riot of 1965 — the McCone Commis-

9

sion), and Communist agitators (George Wallace during the presidential campaign of 1968). The National Advisory Commission on Civil Disorders (Kerner Commission), on the other hand, found "no evidence that all or any of the disorders [of 1967] or the incidents that led to them were planned or directed by any organization or group, international, national or local"; and similar findings have been made with respect to virtually every major racial outbreak of the 1960's.[3] Moreover, the Kerner Report demonstrated conclusively that the typical rioter was *not* a member of a criminal, unemployed or migrant "underclass," while other studies have documented the positive responses of black nonrioters towards the uprisings.[4] In April 1968 one could not find a black political leader of consequence ready to condemn the disorders following Dr. King's assassination.

The strategy of attributing violent eruptions to small, unrepresentative minorities in order to vindicate the existing political structure is as old as America. Indian revolts of the late eighteenth and early nineteenth centuries were said to be the work of British agents, slave revolts were attributed by southerners to abolitionist spies, and unnamed Confederate plotters were accused of fomenting the New York draft riot of 1863. Employers consistently blamed violent strikes on "foreign agitators" or "anarchist conspirators," while anarchists of a more modern variety were said to have provoked antiwar disturbances at the 1968 national Democratic convention and elsewhere. In each of these cases (as well as in others discussed later) those in power have understated the militancy of a large group in order to justify suppression of the violent vanguard. Where the violent actors constitute a group too large to be considered a "tiny minority," however, this dodge will not work, and a new description is trotted out.

Now mass violence becomes "mob hysteria" and is dismissed as irrational.

This characterization, like the theories of outside agitation and minority incitement, is intended to deprive violent uprisings of political content by characterizing them as a form of evil or madness. (Note, for example, the emphasis of the McCone Commission on enraged mobs, and the commonly accepted theory of assassination as the work of isolated lunatics.) Discarding the myth of peaceful progress, however, one sees that mass violence may be both irrational *and* political, or, more accurately, that the academic distinction between "expressive" and "instrumental" violence is often irrelevant in practice. The enraged, drunken, paranoid Irish rioters of New York had reason, in 1863, to attack conscription offices administering an unjust draft law, stores which exploited them, policemen who oppressed them, and Negroes who broke their strikes and took their jobs. Their immensely destructive uprising was based on the communal recognition (by no means irrational) that their only real power was the power to disrupt; they had no other resource. Much the same may be said of ghetto blacks in the 1960's. "Even paranoids," as the joke goes, "have real enemies."

Liberation from the myth also permits fresh consideration of the vexing question of the "violent minority." Do the rioters, strikers or guerrillas "represent" their groups, or are they acting on their own, contrary to the expressed wishes or best interests of their people? The matter is extremely complex, since between the Ku Klux Klan, for example, which probably did represent the wishes of most white southerners after the Civil War, and the pro-German Bundists of the late 1930's, who represented only themselves, there is an infinite number of possible gradations.

11

More important, the question as stated is misleading, since the concept of representation (a product of rationalist political thinking) is hardly adequate to explain the relationship between militant activists and more passive members of a politically developing group. Clearly, the farmers of Pennsylvania in the 1790's were "represented" both by the Whiskey Rebels, who led them into insurrection, and by President Washington, who suppressed the rebellion. American blacks in the 1960's are "represented" both by the machine politicians who often get their votes and by the Black Panther party, which symbolizes the spirit of black pride and resistance to oppression. In most cases of large-scale, sustained political violence one finds that the violent minority "represents" a much larger group, although not necessarily in the traditional rationalist sense.

This is true, incidentally, even where there is intimidation of nonviolent group members by the militants. The charge of intimidation is almost always provable, since violent revolts are usually (and sometimes primarily) directed against "collaborators"— members of the insurgent group believed to be in league with outside enemies. The principal activity of the pre-Revolutionary Sons of Liberty was intimidation, and threats against alleged collaborators were characteristic of farmer uprisings, southern terrorism, labor violence, and both immigrant group and racial disorders thereafter. Once politics moves onto the plane of violence the maxim often followed is, "Those who are not with us are against us"; waverers are frequently assisted in making their choice by physical and economic threats and ostracism. Since this is characteristic of many violent uprisings, however, it does not help to determine the legitimacy, from the point of view of the group, of particular revolts. A more sophisticated analysis is necessary which, accepting a degree of intimidation as characteristic, goes on to determine the extent to which particular episodes or campaigns of political violence correspond to the perceived interests and felt needs of particular groups.

So long as one subscribes to the myth of peaceful progress, however, this analysis cannot be made. The charge of intimidation, like that of outside agitation or minority incitement, and the epithets "unnecessary," "useless" and "un-American" are not meant to further one's understanding of violent uprisings but to authorize their suppression. Like most in-group ideologies, the myth of peaceful progress is intended at bottom to legitimize authority and permit conscience-free suppression of protest. By insisting that group revolt is produced by lawlessness, irrationality, impatience or malice, it serves the traditional function of helping those at the top to be comfortable with their power, secure in the knowledge that those at the bottom deserve to be there. Conversely, reading the myth into American history provides groups which have "made it" into the middle class with a justification-by-contrast. *"We* escaped from *our* ghettos without resorting to violence," they proudly claim. The implication, of course, is that groups which rose from poverty and powerlessness without participating in riots or revolts are somehow superior or are better Americans than those who did not. "Nobody gave us anything," runs the almost liturgical refrain. "We earned our position by working for it." Two considerations, however, collapse this comfortable mythic structure.

(1) Groups cannot be classified as "violent" or "nonviolent." Most domestic groups, including those which rose to power during and after the New Deal, participated at times in political or social movements productive of disorder. Farmer uprisings are part of our national heritage; as late as the 1930's debt-ridden farmers were blocking mortgage foreclosures, burning crops, and buying in fore-

closed properties for pennies at "shotgun sales." Working-men struggling to unionize were even more accustomed to using violence to gain their objectives; as Philip Taft has remarked, no nation has a bloodier history of labor-management conflict than the United States.[5] Businessmen hired private armies of their own or allied themselves with gangsters to defeat the union movement. And immigrants in urban areas fought each other and the police for control of the streets, participated in race riots, and engaged in a style of politics not meant for those with weak stomachs or weak fists. They created organized crime in the United States and (as Daniel Bell has suggested) used criminal activity both as a way of exercising community control and as a road to economic advancement when other routes were closed.[6] The same groups which began their rise to suburban respectability and middle-of-the road politics in the 1930's and 1940's were the Molly Maguires, Wobblies, gangsters and anarchists of an earlier age. But they did not hesitate, once power had been obtained, to employ "official violence" through control of local government and the police against emerging groups now as violence-prone as they once had been.

Naturally, members of the ultra-respectable labor movement of the 1960's do not like to be reminded of the AFL dynamiters of 1910–1920, the Kentucky border mining wars of the 1920's or the violent CIO strikes of the 1930's. Neither do Irish Americans customarily reminisce about New York's Five Points gang or the draft riots, the Molly Maguire terrorist movement or the mob scenes formerly enacted in Boston's South End. Italian Americans are sensitive about their forebears' connections with organized crime, construction contract graft and union racketeering; and regularly omitted from the standard histories of "Famous Jewish Americans" are the names of famous

Jewish anarchists, Communists, gangsters and machine politicians. All oppressed economic, ethnic and religious groups, of course, are subject to discrimination and racist stereotyping. But in their zeal to liberate themselves from racist stereotypes, groups which have now "arrived" are inclined to forget that in America, freedom, prosperity and social status are not handed over politely to newcomers, nor are they simply earned by individual effort. They are fought for and taken, often by methods every bit as violent and dirty as those used by the power structure to keep newcomers "in their place."

(2) Although the distinction between "violent" and "nonviolent" groups is without historical foundation, it is nevertheless clear that some groups rose much more rapidly and painlessly than others. The experience of various domestic groups may be thought of as ranging along a continuum of participation in violent behavior, from sporadic, local and inchoately political outbreaks (for example, gang warfare) to sustained, consciously political revolts on a national scale (for example, armed rebellion). Thus, Jews participated in gang warfare and labor violence but not in major riots; unionists in labor violence and riots but not in sustained uprisings on a national scale; blacks in successive riots nationally but not in widespread guerrilla terrorism; Indians and post–Civil War southerners in terrorism and partial military mobilization; and patriots, loyalists, northerners and southerners in massive military mobilization, or "war." In some cases — for example, labor-management violence — sporadic local outbreaks over a long period of time proved even more destructive than more formalized revolt.

At the outset, one thing seems clear: those groups which achieved success without participating in sustained rioting, guerrilla terrorism or outright insurrection were not necessarily more talented, hardworking or "American" than those that resorted to higher levels of violence. The resistance of more powerful groups to change is one key determinant of the degree of violence produced by group struggle; another is the match between out-group characteristics and the needs of a changing political-economic system. The immigrants of 1880–1920 were fortunate in arriving in the United States during the greatest period of industrial growth in the nation's history. An industrializing economy needed strong backs, even the backs of Italian or Polish peasant farmers. A population fleeing from farm to city needed the services of urban entrepreneurs, even the services of Irish barkeeps and Jewish tailors. A vast increase in jobs permitted almost every group to get "a piece of the action," if not through labor unionism or politics then through strikebreaking and racketeering. A still decentralized political system permitted new arrivals to take control of urban machines and state legislatures, and the Great Depression would create an even rarer opportunity for advancement by generating a radical political realignment on the national level. The newcomers might sometimes be impelled to resort to violence against forces slowing their advance — scabs, bosses, rival street gangs or competing political organizations — but the environment, itself in flux, yielded to their efforts. The nation was being transformed from top to bottom, and they were part of the transformation.

Imagine, on the other hand, what life would be like for Irish or Italian farmers entering American port cities today. Even without the disadvantage of being black, they would find themselves in much the same position as that of the rural Negroes who entered northern cities in the millions between 1940 and 1960. Even immigrants with an urban outlook, like the Puerto Ricans, find their mobility

16

significantly reduced in an age of giant corporations and postindustrial automation. The "mature economy" clearly works against such emerging groups, much as the "immature economy" of the turn of the century worked for them. The economic growth rate slows down; labor unions monopolize jobs and multiply apprenticeship requirements; small businesses and family farms become obsolete; businesses raise educational and professional standards for employment, and the low rate of unemployment "acceptable" to economists is multiplied five to ten times among the disadvantaged. What this means to emerging groups is an enormous increase in dependence upon governments and powerful private interests, for it is their good will rather than the operations of the free market which decides whether they will be included in the mature economy. And, as we will see, there is an important relationship in America between group dependence and group violence.

The same scenario is played out on the political level as well, with powerlessness and dependence feeding each other in this most vicious of vicious cycles. In place of the business elite which confronted older immigrant groups there has existed since the age of Franklin D. Roosevelt a more broadly based ruling coalition which includes, besides big business, elements of such former out-groups as unionists, farmers and many of the immigrants of 1880–1920. Ironically — since these are the groups most wedded to the myth of peaceful progress and the culpability of the violent — it is the existence of this coalition, exercising power through a highly centralized federal bureaucracy, which helps keep emerging groups powerless and dependent. This point is critical to an understanding of the recent changes in American life most productive of violence: the Roosevelt revolution was *not* a continuing revolution. The redistribution of power in the United States which was effected between 1935 and 1945 did not continue after the end of World War II. As a result, the ins were frozen in and the outs out. However, as stated earlier, no domestic group in our success-oriented society has been content to remain frozen out merely for the sake of domestic peace.

Those whom the New Deal brought to power have not appreciated this; hence, they do not understand why the disadvantaged and excluded resort to violence. They remember their own almost miraculous rise to respectability and national influence, and assume that the out-groups of 1968 have the same opportunity to succeed. Themselves holders of power, they are unable to perceive their own resistance to political change. Because the new ruling coalition is more representative than the older elite, its members can believe that it is literally "democratic" — representative of all the people: "We have arrived; therefore, America has arrived." This fallacy recapitulates a tragic error — the identification of the American dream with present reality. And this, of course, is precisely what the myth of peaceful progress is intended to accomplish. The characterization of America as a peacefully self-transforming system leaves no room for violent protest, which by definition falls outside the system. Eden is not Eden unless he who rebels is an original sinner.

It is important, on the other hand, not to misuse history by asserting that violence always works, or is always necessary. Clearly, this would be to create a new myth — a myth of violent progress — which could be disposed of easily by citing examples of violence with no group advancement (like the American Indian revolts) and advancement with comparatively little violence (as among American Jews). The point, really, is that political and economic power is not as easily shared, or turned over to powerless outsiders, as has been thought. Because of their size, degree of absolute or relative deprivation, and relationship to more powerful forces, the demands of some domestic groups for equality and power have been impossible to meet within the context of *existing* political and economic arrangements. To admit Indian tribes, or members of labor unions, or the mass of oppressed black people to full membership in American society meant that existing systems would have to be transformed, at least in part, to make room for the previously excluded; and that in the transformation, land-hungry settlers, large corporations, and urban political machines and commercial interests, respectively, would have to give ground. Transformation and concomitant power realignments were refused in the first case, granted (only partially and after great social disorder) in the second, and are in doubt in the third. The moral is not that America is a "sick society" (what a curiously prideful claim that is!) but that, like all other societies, it has failed to solve the oldest problem of politics — the problem of nonviolent power transference.

One further bit of comparative history may make this clearer. President Rutherford B. Hayes, a Republican, helped to break the railroad strikes of 1877. President Grover Cleveland, a Democrat, almost singlehandedly broke the railroad strike of 1894. As a result, union leaders like Eugene V. Debs realized that, from their point of view, it did not matter which party was in power. The transference of formal political power from Republicans to Democrats was a mere ritual, disguising the fact that the same interests effectively controlled both parties. The plight of American blacks in modern times, faced by conservative business opposition among Republicans and conservative union opposition among Democrats, with both parties bidding for southern support, is comparable. Third party politics, to be sure, was one method by which large excluded groups sometimes attempted to force a system transformation, but the technique was rarely effective, given the strength of the American Center and its systematic discrimination against minority parties. It was when such desperation tactics proved useless that the probability of mass political violence was highest, for no large American group, to my knowledge, gave up the struggle for admission to power without a fight. Nor have the holders of power, from George III of Britain to Mayor Richard Daley of Chicago, meekly stood by while upstarts challenged their hard-won preeminence.

Many Americans recognize inwardly that the dream of peaceful system transformation and nonviolent power sharing *is* a dream — a utopia yet unachieved — and this recognition helps to explain why we have not machine-gunned black rioters or student demonstrators. For if mass violence were always un-American, unnecessary and useless, as official rhetoric claims, the correct response would be to crush it, immediately and brutally. Instead, half realizing that riots and insurrections imply a failure of the dream, our initial reaction is that of George Washington, upon hearing of the Shays Rebellion: "If they have *real* grievances, redress them, if possible; or acknowledge the justice of them and your inability to do so at the moment. If they have not, employ the force of Government against them at once . . ." [7] The difficulty arises, however, when well-intended reforms do not lead to a redress of grievances, and violence continues. The result may be the escalation of both rebellion and suppression to the level of open warfare.

Major Revolts i

Disposing of the myth of peaceful progress sets the stage for reconsideration of the role which mass political violence has played in American history. Immediately, however, there arise profound problems of definition. Does "violence" refer only to acts causing personal injury or property damage, or does the term include threats and other forms of coercion, such as those exercised by government? Does "political" refer only to acts undertaken in conscious pursuance of an express political program, or does the adjective describe a wider range of phenomena — for example, "spontaneous" mob action or the enforcement of controversial laws? American history contains an enormous amount of activity which may justifiably be called both violent and political, even though in many instances we are not accustomed to think about it in these terms. For example, criminal activity (both organized and unorganized) has often been a means of advanc-

22

American History

ing group interests and influencing government. Vigilante movements of various kinds, although purporting to restore law and order, almost always attempt to secure power for certain groups and deny it to others. Family feuds and range wars have frequently been as political as they have been violent. And what is the enforcement of laws which favor or punish particular groups but another form of political violence?

Clearly, this is not just a problem of definition but also of philosophy. Adopting narrow definitions of both violence and politics, those who wish to minimize the significance of violence in American history can limit the discussion to a few well-known episodes like the American Revolution and the Civil War, while those wishing to emphasize our violent past can just as easily paint a picture of omnipresent and unremitting conflict by utilizing the widest possible definitions. In this discussion we accept a broad definition in theory, but limit the discussion in practice. Violence, for us, includes threats, coercion and physical damage to persons or property; political violence is violence resorted to by or on behalf of groups, involving collective action, and related to competition for political or economic power. But our principal concern is with episodes of political violence involving politically, economically and socially disadvantaged "out-groups" — episodes so clearly related to such groups' struggles for power as to merit the name "revolts." With the definitional problem shelved, if not solved, we can proceed to describe in summary form some of the major domestic revolts, and then to examine their implications.[1]

Indian Revolts

Beginning early in the seventeenth century American Indians engaged in a series of violent uprisings aimed at securing their land and liberty against invasion by white settlers. Britain's victory over France in the 1760's triggered the great revolt of the eastern tribes known as Pontiac's Conspiracy, and American independence was followed by Little Turtle's War, the Blackhawk War, the revolt of the Creeks and Cherokees and the Seminole War — vain attempts to resist the thrust of white settlement and Indian "removal" to territory west of the Mississippi. (Removal of the eastern Indians was carried out by federal and state governments with great violence and brutality in the 1830's and 1840's.) For the Indians of the West who fought in the post–Civil War rebellions of the Sioux, Sac and Fox, Navajo, Apache and other tribes, the price of defeat was the loss not only of land but also of liberty and livelihood. The result, as we know, was decimation of the Indian people and the triumph of the official reservation policy. Calling these conflicts "wars" against Indian "nations," of course, does not alter their character: they were armed insurrections by domestic groups denied the privileges of citizenship as well as the perquisites of nationhood. For more than a century after its creation, suppressing Indian revolts was the chief occupation of the United States Army. The use of antiquated terminology to describe excesses of official violence (death marches are called "removals" and concentration camps "reservations") has obscured the analogy with more recent episodes of near genocide.

Appalachian Farmers' Revolts

Small debtor farmers living in the western regions of the coastal states participated in numerous disorders from the 1740's, when New Jerseyites refused to pay their rents and Massachusetts men marched on Boston in support of a land bank law, until the 1790's, when Pennsylvania farmers and mountain men fomented the Whiskey and Fries rebellions. In a series of revolts now known by such names as the Wars of the Regulators (North and South Carolina), the War of the New Hampshire Grants (New York–Vermont), the Shays Rebellion (Massachusetts) and the Whiskey Rebellion (Pennsylvania and neighboring states), debtor farmers protested half a century of economic exploitation, political exclusion and social discrimination by their East Coast rulers. In state after state, hated laws provoked first civil disobedience, then physical attacks on tax collectors and other law enforcers, and finally the closing down of courts to prevent issuance of mortgage foreclosures and indictments. Rejecting compromises proffered by eastern legislatures, the rebels established *de facto* control over the western counties of several states, lasting in some cases for several years. Although most insurgent groups were defeated and dispersed by superior military force, the *series* of revolts did not end until Jefferson's election provided access to the political system and new land created fresh economic opportunity. Where the political and economic systems were especially rigid, as in the Hudson Valley in New York, agitation and sporadic violence continued well into the nineteenth century.

Civil Strife During the Revolutionary Period

The American colonists, as we know, gained their independence from Britain after a decade of civil strife and six years of revolutionary war. What is now becoming clearer is the extent to which the struggle pitted Americans against Americans, with insurgents resorting to modes of political violence and authorities to modes of repression which were repeated again in later "independence" revolts. The first decade, beginning with the stamp tax controversy, saw a steady rise in civil disorder in the form of massive civil disobedience, urban rioting, economic boycotts, sabotage of government property, terrorist attacks on officials, and finally military organization — paralleled, of course, by simultaneous escalation of suppression attempts by the authorities and their local supporters. Small, militant groups like the Sons of Liberty and, later, the Committees of Correspondence organized campaigns against British colonial legislation, directing both economic and physical coercion against merchants who refused to participate in boycotts of British goods. With the outbreak of hostilities against the British, civil strife increased in both intensity and scope, spreading into rural areas like New Jersey and South Carolina, where roving guerrilla bands played nightmare games of armed hide-and-seek. Negroes and Indians were often pawns in these exercises, whose excesses — as emigrating Tories realized — would not necessarily be confined to the period of formal hostilities. Generated by a justifiable fear of reprisals, the massive Tory emigration which began in the last years of the war probably helped to prevent the sort of prolonged revolutionary violence and emigré retaliation which characterized the French Revolution.

The Southern Rebellion

In the years between 1820 and 1860 white southerners became, in Jesse T. Carpenter's words, "a conscious minority" — a development highly productive of political violence in every section of the nation.[2] This was the period in which southerners committed themselves to an agricultural system based on slave breeding and plantation farming; in which the dream of emancipation fled the South and became the exclusive property of northern abolitionists; in which thinkers like John C. Calhoun constructed vain theoretical defenses against increasing northern power while others, with a pride born of desperation, dreamed the "purple dream" of a southern empire stretching from the Mason-Dixon Line to Tierra del Fuego. Like rebellious domestic groups before and after them, white southerners moved from sporadic civil disobedience (the nullification controversy of 1828–1830) to terrorism by proxy (in the Kansas-Nebraska war) and finally to outright armed rebellion. The North, whose intense antiabolitionism initially resulted in violence against leading abolitionists like William Lloyd Garrison and Elijah Lovejoy, eventually followed the same pattern, from mass disobedience after passage of the fugitive slave laws to the fielding of a settler army in Kansas, and from support for John Brown's raid on Harpers Ferry to the election of a President committed to the preservation of the Union by force. We will have more to say later about the southern rebellion and northern response.

Guerrilla Warfare in the Postwar South

Less familiar is the struggle, after the surrender at Appomattox, waged by southern terrorist groups, the most powerful being the Ku Klux Klan. During Reconstruction (especially after 1867) the South was treated as occupied territory; large numbers of her men were disenfranchised and the law was upheld by occupying armies. More important, the southern economy remained shattered, Reconstruction governments were considered illegitimate by most whites, and the social system, formerly based on absolute white supremacy, seemed to be falling apart. The Klan's purposes — to prevent Negroes from voting or participating in politics, restore the substance of the prewar southern social and economic system, and drive "carpetbagger" officials and their "scalawag" collaborators out of the South — were substantially realized by 1871, when Congress first legislated against the Klan, and entirely realized in 1876, when President Hayes withdrew the last of the northern troops. The conflict was waged according to principles of guerrilla warfare which have since been codified by Mao Tse-tung, Ho Chi Minh and others — use of a sympathetic civilian population to shelter the insurgents, avoidance of open battles, politicization of the rebel army, and so forth. This was the first large-scale guerrilla war fought in the United States, and the only one in which the guerrillas were entirely successful. Unwilling to pay the very high price of suppressing a popular insurgency, the North simply acquiesced in the return of white supremacy to the unrepentant South.

Labor-Management Warfare

Following the Civil War, workingmen attempting to organize for collective action engaged in more than half a century of violent warfare with industrialists, their private armies, and unemployed workers used to break strikes. The anthracite fields of western Pennsylvania were Molly Maguire territory during the 1870's. After losing a coal strike early in the period, the predominantly Irish Mollys sought to regain control of the area by systematic use of violence, including sabotage and assassination, and were successful until penetrated and exposed by a Pinkerton spy. In 1877, unorganized railroad workers protesting wage cuts, the use of scabs and probable loss of their jobs during a depression engaged in a series of immensely destructive riots across the nation, with Baltimore and Pittsburgh hardest hit; the total cost in life and property during these riots has never been accurately estimated. Violent conflict in heavy industry and transportation continued with the Haymarket Square bombing (1886), the Homestead strike at Carnegie Steel (and a subsequent anarchist attempt in 1892 to kill Carnegie president Henry Clay Frick), the Pullman strike, which became particularly violent after President Cleveland called in federal troops over the protest of the governor of Illinois (1894), the bombing of the *Los Angeles Times* building by persons associated with the AFL (1910), the IWW-led textile strike at Lowell, Massachusetts (1912), and national strikes against railroads and steel, with troops called out in several cities (1919) — to name just a few of the most disruptive and best-known battles. Meanwhile, in the mining and timber industries of the West, an initial blow-up in the Coeur d'Alene region of Idaho (1892) was followed by twenty years of the most intense and sanguinary struggle, ranging from Goldfield, Nevada, and Ludlow, Colorado, to the West Virginia–Kentucky border. On the eve of implementation of the pro-union Wagner Act ten striking workers from Republic Steel were shot and killed by management forces in Chicago; additional gunfire and death accompanied the efforts of CIO auto workers to occupy Michigan automobile plants by "sitting down." Legislative transformation of labor-management relations ended this principal period of labor war in the United States, although violent incidents accompanying hard-fought strikes seem now a part of our "way of life."

Urban Rioting and Ethnic Revolts

Beginning in the 1840's and 1850's and continuing after the Civil War, the United States was transformed by successive waves of immigration, principally from Europe, into the major cities of the North. The result was an enormous increase in urban political violence, not *by* the newly arrived immigrants so much as *against* them, as older groups attempted to protect their political power, property values and life styles against the onslaught. Thus, white Anglo-Saxon Protestant workingmen, organized politically as Native Americans, tore the Irish section of Philadelphia apart in 1844; similar anti-Irish riots occurred in Baltimore, Boston and other port cities. On the West Coast, Chinese and Japanese immigrants were the victims of systematic persecution, including mob violence and lynchings, throughout the 1860's and 1870's. As Italians were lynched in New Orleans and Jews attacked in New York, the newer immigrant groups learned to defend themselves by organizing paramilitary street gangs which engaged in continuous limited war in defense of shifting group territory. In some instances, as when blacks or new immigrants were protected by big business and city governments, nativist violence took on the characteristics of anti-authority rebellion. This was the case, for example, when New York's Irish population simultaneously attacked Lincoln's draft offices, New York's Negro population, the homes and shops of the rich, and the New York police in the immensely destructive draft riot of 1863. It was also the case in 1877, when San Francisco workingmen rioting in sympathy with railroad strikers battled both police and Chinese immigrants. In fact, it is virtually impossible to segregate into neat categories "nativist," "labor" and "race" rioting, since in most cases older (but still insecure) domestic groups were reacting simultaneously to economic, political and cultural threats posed by newcomers. Strife between the working class and the "underclass" seems to be one of the more permanent features of American capitalism.

Black Revolt

During the years of slavery black Americans participated in at least 250 abortive insurrections, the best known of which were the Gabriel, Vesey and Nat Turner insurrections. After the Civil War they were the victims of white attacks, better described as massacres than as riots, in dozens of cities ranging from Cincinnati (1886) to East St. Louis (1917). Black immigration into northern cities following World War I, however, generated riots in which blacks and whites fought with equal fervor for the control of disputed territory; in dozens of cities such as Chicago and Washington, D.C. (1919), Tulsa (1921), New York (Harlem, 1935) and Detroit (1943) the races warred, each side avenging attack with reprisal. But starting with the Harlem uprising of 1943 — and continuing after the great postwar emigration to northern cities with Rochester and Philadelphia (1964), Los Angeles (Watts, 1965), Chicago and Cleveland (1966), Newark, northern New Jersey cities and Detroit (1967), Washington, D.C., Pittsburgh and Chicago (1968), not to mention numerous smaller outbreaks in other cities — blacks resorted to a different sort of violence. These were spontaneous mass uprisings directed not so much against white persons as against white-owned property and those representing an oppressive legal order — policemen, firemen and National Guardsmen. By 1969, there was some evidence that this phase of the revolt was ending (at least in the larger northern cities). Increasingly bitter conflict between politicized law enforcement forces and militant street groups in Chicago, New York, San Francisco, Cleveland, Philadelphia and elsewhere raised the possibility that a new phase of the revolt in the North might be beginning.

Student Revolt in the 1960's

The Free Speech Movement at the University of California at Berkeley in 1964 initiated a wave of campus uprisings which has not yet ended. Radical students, nonstudents and faculty members at hundreds of colleges and universities participated in direct action against university administrations and in mass demonstrations and civil disobedience in protest of the Vietnam War. Generally, "movement" action did not include physical attacks on persons, but was limited to public acts of civil disobedience, strikes, occupation of buildings and demonstrations; at times it included symbolic imprisonment of university administrators or representatives of the military establishment and, occasionally, destruction of property. On several college campuses, such as the University of California at Berkeley, Columbia University and San Francisco State College, and in certain cities like Washington, D.C. (1967) and Chicago (1968), the calling out of police or military forces in response to such activities resulted in significant escalations of the level of violence, with law enforcement forces taking punitive physical action against large numbers of demonstrators. The student uprisings generally lacked leadership and organization; what leadership there was was provided by members of groups like the Students for a Democratic Society, which initially demanded an end to the Vietnam War and to university involvement with military and business interests supporting the war, as well as an increase in student influence in the administration of particular universities. In certain instances, as at Howard, Northwestern and San Francisco State, the principal motivation for revolt was student demand for redefinition of university attitudes and policies toward blacks. But generally the insurgent students were white and upper middle class in origin. Participants in a cultural revolution, they challenged not only the legitimacy of existing political bureaucracies but also the validity of existing cultural norms and ethical practices in the United States. In 1969 the ideological gap between young radicals and their opponents seemed to be widening rather than narrowing. While SDS declared itself a revolutionary movement, several states and the United States Congress considered legislation to punish student demonstrators, and California governor Ronald Reagan unleashed the combined forces of three law enforcement agencies on the students of Berkeley, revolutionary and nonrevolutionary alike.

For now, the catalogue is completed. Later we shall consider in greater detail some of the specific episodes dealt with summarily here; immediately, the question is what to make of these recurrent mass revolts. Shall we merely remark (as is now the fashion) that America has been "a violent society," or is there something more that can be said about the nature of out-group revolt in the United States? Obviously, there is no one interpretation which will explain all manifestations of domestic political violence from lynchings to violent strikes and from Indian raids to race riots. Still, after analyzing the violent political movements briefly described above, it is difficult to escape the conclusion that *patterns* of violence exist — that many outbreaks of domestic revolt, although separated in time and place, share certain common characteristics. Indeed, it seems that responses to mass violence may also be patterned — in fact, that many of the most significant outbreaks reflect similar relationships between less powerful and more powerful domestic groups. One pattern which seems particularly relevant in the light of contemporary events is elucidated here.

From Appalachian farmers of the 1760's to urban blacks of the 1960's some out-groups resorted to, or were driven to, mass violence in the form of civil disobedience, rioting, terrorism or armed insurrection. This is clear, but it leaves unanswered a critical question: why have some groups revolted while others have not? For example, for decades after Reconstruction, southern blacks, although excluded from politics, denied the most elementary human rights, lynched and massacred, did not turn to organized violence. Was this because they were so utterly outmanned and outgunned? Perhaps, but so were generations of American Indians who fought on nonetheless; and so were the Watts and Detroit rioters of the 1960's. Was it, as some have suggested, because until the late 1950's Negroes had insufficient hope, because the "revolution of rising expectations" had not occurred? Perhaps, but other groups which *did* experience a revolution of rising expectations while suffering great deprivation — for example, western farmers during the 1870's and 1880's — continued to engage in more or less nonviolent politics without resort to mass rioting. Was it then, as others have said, because the southern social system was stable, and in it Negroes had "their place"? Perhaps, but why did blacks accept that place in 1890 while white workingmen of the same era were refusing to accept theirs? Perhaps most blacks were passive because they were not conscious of their deprivation relative to whites; they were uneducated and there were, after all, more poor whites than poor blacks. But this also is unsatisfactory; it fails to tell us what creates a consciousness of relative deprivation and why groups quite conscious of their relative powerlessness — like the eastern European immigrants of the early 1900's — did not revolt.

Indeed, none of these static theories of social behavior will tell us what we want to know, why some groups and not others participated in mass revolt. Such theories are often advanced by scholars observing violent group behavior, who note, for example, that Group A has recently experienced a revolution of rising expectations, or that Group B's members are newly conscious of their relative deprivation. The scholars generally dodge the question whether these factors, singly or in combination, will always, or even sometimes, produce a violent revolt, or else they hedge by disclaiming an intention to generalize. Furthermore, they frequently ignore the existence of violent outbreaks which do not seem to be produced by *any* of the above factors — outbreaks such as that of the Chicago police during the Democratic national convention in 1968, when (according to the report of the Walker fact-finding commission to the National Advisory Commission on the Causes and Prevention of Violence) policemen disobeying orders created a "police riot" in order to punish demonstrators. The need, then, is to get away from factor analysis, and instead to describe the *process* which generates either violent or nonviolent group behavior.

One observes, for example, that group revolts in the United States seldom seem "revolutionary." Rarely, if ever, does a domestic group in revolt attack the powers-that-be at their source. In the 1770's and 1780's Appalachian farmers mounted no Tet offensive against eastern cities; they merely shut down local courts and drove judges and tax collectors out of their territory. Southern terrorists did not attempt to overthrow the government at Washington (the constitution of the Ku Klux Klan began with a declaration of allegiance to the United States government). They ran carpetbaggers and scalawags *out* of the South and reasserted by force their dominion over native blacks. Even militant labor unionists did not foment (or come close to fomenting) a socialist revolution. They resorted to violence against local enemies and symbols of oppression like scabs, Pinkerton men and company property, but did not ordinarily attack employers in person or federal troops. And urban ethnic groups, fighting each other or the cops, or looting the "outsider's" store, did not dream of establishing a Paris Commune. To establish control over their own territories and their own lives seemed sufficient.

In fact, it seems that domestic mass violence has often involved attempts to drive invaders off the out-group's soil, and to assert or reassert the group's control over its own affairs. In this respect, the American Revolution was archetypical. Many subsequent revolts, including agrarian uprisings, nativist rioting, the terrorism of the first Klan, some manifestations of labor violence and the black uprisings of the 1960's, have been in the direction of independence.

"Independence!" The idea, in one form or another, has motivated rebels as diverse as Tom Paine and John Adams, John Brown and Jefferson Davis, Tom Watson and Robert Williams. A drive toward independence (which those in power call "secession") was frequently the last resort of large, culturally cohesive domestic groups which believed themselves doomed to perpetual dependence or extinction within the larger society. It inflamed Kentucky and Tennessee farmers in the 1790's, New England businessmen during the War of 1812, white southern nationalists in the nineteenth century and black northern nationalists in the twentieth. In a less extreme and legalistic form the urge for self-determination has motivated both violent and nonviolent political movements. *De facto* independence within a *de jure* nation was the goal of the southerners who created the Ku Klux Klan and the westerners who created the Grange, the European immigrants who invented the modern political machine and the African immigrants who invented the ideology of black power. Indeed, in calling for some form of independence American rebels are able to demand drastic transformations of American society while remaining squarely in the tradition of Patrick Henry and Tom Paine. The ideology of independence permits the rebel to blend radicalism with patriotism.

Analysis of the causes, targets, methods and ideology of major domestic revolts reveals the importance of the theme of independence, particularly in the sense of *de facto* control of local territory, to insurgent out-groups. Very often the theme is not expressed verbally, but in action. For example, the precipitating or triggering causes of many domestic revolts are legal acts carried out by agents of a central authority on the territory of an out-group. These are seen by members of the group as intolerable invasions of the group *dominium,* which explicitly or implicitly deny local autonomy. In such cases the insurgency is initially a spontaneous mass response aimed at getting the representatives of authority (and their local collaborators) out of the territory. This was the case when western farmers counterattacked against eastern revenue agents and court officials; when the Sons of Liberty forced stamp tax collectors to resign and pro-British merchants to close shop; when southerners fought to rid their section of carpetbaggers and scalawags; when New York Irishmen closed down draft offices; when racists attacked civil rights workers and bombed churches, and when urban blacks attacked policemen and burned white-owned ghetto stores to the ground. Moreover, even where this type of group violence became less spontaneous and mob-dominated, more calculated and organized, it was generally limited to the original locus of conflict — the out-group's territory. This may seem startling in view of the common assumption that violence tends to spread unless met by counterforce; but it is true nonetheless. Seldom are insurgents so driven by "hysteria" or "insensate rage" as to pursue the outsider onto his own territory. (Even in the case of labor violence, most conflict took place on company property or in company towns.)

Therefore, when we say that the targets of domestic violence have often been agents of authority and local collaborators found on the territory, an important negative is implied: usually such violence is not revolutionary in the traditional sense since central power is not threatened. Rebellious domestic groups rarely pretend to speak for or represent the nation; they speak for themselves, *as* "na-

tions." Locally, they have aimed at replacing "alien domination" with some form of "self-rule," a goal which leads
more logically to decentralization of power than to a revolution at the center. For this reason, the ideology of domestic insurrection has generally not included plans for the
transformation of politics or the economy on a national
level. In fact, major ideological declarations have often followed rather than preceded revolt, serving more to ration-
alize past action than to incite future rebellion. Tom
Paine's *Common Sense* justified the colonial revolt which
had begun following passage of the Stamp Act; the socialism of the IWW was the product rather than the cause of
labor-management conflict; and, in our own time, the ideology of black power was created *after* the ghetto uprisings
of 1964–66 had taken place.

Black power illustrates a second characteristic of independence ideologies: their lack of "ideological" content in
the traditional European sense. Whereas European ideologies proceed from a philosophy of history to a vision of
social transformation, American ideologies more often
proceed from a sense of group identity to a vision of independence. This means, first, that thinkers like Paine,
Jefferson and Calhoun, not to mention Malcolm X and Eldridge Cleaver, devoted a great deal of argument and
energy to *defining* the group seeking autonomy, and increasing its nation-consciousness. (Leaders of the New
Left spend as much time discussing the need for radical community as the need for a radical program.) Second,
it means that rebel leaders generally do *not* define with any
particularity their vision of the new society; independence, whether literally intended or used as a metaphor for
increased local autonomy, becomes an end in itself. Indeed, groups seeking independence, or increased collective
power, have often adopted whatever utopia was accepted

39

by the society at large rather than constructing an alternative. The critical question "Independence for what?" has usually not been answered prior to its achievement. The result, at least in the European sense, has been nonrevolutionary ideology, although (as discussed later in Chapter 8) a *coalition* of insurgent groups may demand changes which are in fact revolutionary.

The traditional weapons of domestic revolt have been directed to the same end — maximizing group autonomy. Looting, arson, the beating or humiliation of persons, threats and whisper campaigns, economic boycotts and occasionally use of arms are all aimed at ridding the territory of group enemies or silencing collaborators. For this reason, intimidation has always been a favorite tactic of domestic insurgents. A man ridden out of town on a rail will usually not return; neither will a merchant burned out of the ghetto. Moreover, since central authority is not attacked directly, the use of such weapons forces the authorities to respond (if at all) by making a real "invasion" of the group's territory, thereby solidifying insurgency and escalating the level of violence. If this occurs, the insurgents can be counted upon to counterescalate by resorting to more calculated, organized, selective and aggressive force directed against the occupying forces, whether state militia, carpetbagger troops or white policemen. The weapons and tactics of domestic rebellion speak louder than political ideologies. This message, repeated so often over our three-hundred-year history, is "Get off our backs!"

A great many domestic revolts, then, have been conceived as defensive responses to outside aggression, and have retained their localistic, nonrevolutionary, autonomy-oriented character even after escalation has taken place. Two prerequisites for this type of revolt seem to be a high level of group coherence, usually based on a shared cultural heritage, and a definable territory which can be claimed for the group and protected against "invasion." This sheds some light, perhaps, on the long and violent history of the labor movement, which failed to become revolutionary despite bitter strikes, sporadic terrorism and violent suppression. The labor movement overall lacked both a claimable territory and the group coherence necessary to mount sustained revolts of high intensity; Eugene Debs, for example, attributed failure of the "one big union" movement to labor's ethnic heterogeneity. Conversely, in the isolated mining and timber camps where workers of diverse nationality lived together with their families, a stronger group identity could emerge and there was territory which could be defended from scab invasion. The militancy of the Western Federation of Miners or the old United Mine Workers is therefore attributable to factors other than the personality traits of Big Bill Haywood and John L. Lewis.

The vital twin factors of group coherence and territoriality, however, do not answer the original question: why some groups revolt and others do not. To begin to answer this question it is necessary to describe the relationship between coherent territorial out-groups and groups in power, in order to get a clearer idea of the kind of social change which seems to generate independence revolts. In other words, we must now deal with the underlying causes of such revolts by exploring the question "Independence from what?"

and Inter

Since the opposite of independence is dependence, the prevalence of independence revolts in United States history suggests, *a priori,* a connection between group violence and the consciousness of group dependence. But what sort of dependence are we talking about and how does a group become conscious of it? Why, in an independent society, are some forms of dependence considered intolerable? And how, given the impossibility (for most groups) of securing *literal* independence, is the urge to self-determination satisfied? The evidence suggests that the stage is set for a violent outbreak when a coherent territorial out-group is brought into contact with more aggressive, modernized groups under circumstances causing a simultaneous rise in political consciousness and loss of local autonomy. In plainer English, groups become conscious of their independence when they lose it, and resort to violence when violence seems the only alternative to total

42

3.

Independence
al Colonization

dependence on more powerful groups or individuals. In the process, out-groups seem to pass through certain rough but definable stages of development.

First stage: Relative isolation. The group exists outside the area of economic and political interest of those in positions of great power. While its members are aware of their collective identity (the awareness is often based on shared ethnic characteristics), this group consciousness is not "nationalistic"; that is, it has no political content. Leadership rests with a small elite whose interests are similar to upper-class elites in power. The group's isolation, of course, is not absolute; it may be systematically exploited in certain respects (for example, as a labor force). But on its own territory, where it is generally left alone, it enjoys a high degree of local autonomy and social organization along traditional lines. Examples are Indians of the early seventeenth century, Appalachian farmers and American colonists before 1740, southern whites before 1820, western farmers before 1860, most European immigrant groups during and immediately after their peak years of immigration, urban Negroes before 1920 and Appalachian whites at present.

Second stage: Confrontation. The group is drawn into closer contact with governmental authority and more powerful groups as well as with other out-groups in neighboring territories with whom it engages in conflicts or makes alliances. It begins to pursue political activity along non-violent lines, under middle-class leadership which wishes to integrate its members into the larger society. Group consciousness moves toward the level of "nationalism"; both expectations and dependence vis-à-vis those in power rise. Toward the end of this period the group often makes significant political gains. If, on the local level, its members have achieved sufficient organization to enable them to feel that they can control their own territory and group destiny, it may enter the stage of coalition politics. If, on the other hand, dependence deepens significantly, it begins a revolt. Examples of groups in the confrontation stage are Appalachian farmers between 1730 and 1765, southern whites 1830–1860 and 1865–1867, settled first-generation immigrants, urban blacks 1920–1960, western farmers 1865–1895, Spanish Americans at present.

Third stage: Coalition politics. If the group has secured a local power base either before or after a revolt, it can then enter coalition politics on a national level. If successful, it gains entry into one of the major party coalitions and becomes entitled to share the special privileges of power. If not, it retreats to the local base and awaits its day. Similarly, if the economic needs of the larger society require services which group members are capable of performing, the group will advance to a position of economic power nationally; if not, its members will perform services for each other at the local level. Participation of such "successful" groups in American life involves either a political transformation permitting implementation of group demands or very rapid integration of the group's members individually into the middle class. Examples: German Americans after 1850, Irish Americans after 1880, Jewish Americans after 1930, western farmers after 1935, skilled union members after 1938.

Third stage: Revolt. If, in spite of initial political gains, the group's dependence deepens to the extent that members see themselves losing control over the local power base and slipping into permanent servitude, a resort to violence is predictable. The violence itself often follows a detectable pattern, with individual civil disobedience followed, in order, by mass civil disobedience, marches and demonstrations, spontaneous rioting, and more selective, organized violence. As the group moves through these phases its leadership becomes progressively more militant and the group itself more politically conscious. If the basic problem of group dependence is not resolved, a war of group liberation — which may take the form of mass military mobilization of insurgents or mass acquiescence in guerrilla activity — begins. It does not end until the problem of dependence is solved, either by destruction of the insurgents, victory of the rebellion, or implementation of radical political change. Examples have been given in Chapter 2, but others could be suggested — Hudson Valley farmers during the anti-rent wars of the 1840's, Rhode Islanders during the Dorr Rebellion of the same period, etc.

As we look at the same process from the point of view of groups in power, it becomes apparent that many episodes of domestic revolt have been preceded by periods of

45

rapid social change characterized by increasing contact between them and weak, relatively isolated out-groups. In such periods those with money, power and education — the aggressive, modernizing classes of society — become interested in disadvantaged groups and the territory which they occupy. The key word is "development." To the modernizers, undeveloped land and unexploited markets, unsaved souls and unused human potential are crimes against nature (much as the American Indian's use of potential farmland for hunting seemed sinful to the American colonists). Inexorably, they move in — with investments and merchandise, laws and law enforcement, and often with paternalistic reforms and promises of a brighter future. It is not just capitalistic greed or the missionary spirit which generates this aggression but also modernization itself, uncontrolled. Economic, technological and political integration of the nation make group isolation more and more difficult. Old barriers fall and old boundaries are transgressed. Those in positions of power feel it their *right* to profit or to derive political advantage from the opportunities arising out of "discovery" of a previously isolated group; and they feel it their *duty* (their "white man's burden") to extend to the group the benefits of their law and more advanced culture.

The process is closely analogous to that which, on the international stage, we call colonialism. In fact, it involves the *internal colonization* of less-developed groups, for whom (as for their foreign analogues) it is an exceedingly painful experience. Contact with the modernizers creates hope, ambition and rising expectations and ends the fatalism characteristic of traditional societies. Simultaneously, it creates a new consciousness of group identity and destroys the old group life, generates a desire for power and weakens the group's traditional power base. Not surpris-

46

ingly, if dependence deepens, the group begins to behave like a colonized nation. After all, the internal development of the United States involved the same motivations and pressures, and generated many of the same reactions, as the development of colonial territory by the Great Powers. The perceptions of various out-groups to this effect, although at times overpersonalized and oversimplified, have a basis in fact.

There are fewer differences than one may think between the British or French colonial office and the United States Bureau of Indian Affairs, Freedmen's Bureau or Department of Housing and Urban Development. Like imperial civil servants, our internal colonial administrators have traditionally offered their benighted clients the hope of radical self-improvement while, with the best intentions, they disrupted traditional institutions, siphoned off locally produced wealth to the outside, and bought off the indigenous leadership by trading local power for guarantees of the status quo. The same middle-class church groups which dispatched missionaries to the Africans and Chinese attempted, often simultaneously, to save and "civilize" American Indians, waterfront Irish, eastern European factory workers and ghetto blacks. The same business interests which saw Asia and Latin America as a source of raw materials, cheap labor and potential markets moved to exploit the land, labor and purchasing power of domestic "natives"— Indians, southerners, immigrants or Negroes. The same politicians who set out to democratize the world, American style, extended the benefits of the United States Constitution even to domestic outcasts, while troops used to suppress disorder in the Philippines or Lebanon might also be used to put down revolt in the Coeur d'Alene or Detroit.

Always, the colonizers have had the same dream: unity

and prosperity under one law. Always, the colonized come to the same dream: independence. Thus the predominance in so many domestic revolts of the theme of secession, from the Burr conspiracy and Kentucky and Tennessee secession schemes to the current demand of some black nationalists for a separate territory in the South or West. In the context of internal colonization it is hardly surprising that some domestic revolts have been miniature wars of national liberation. Two illustrations, showing the relationship of revolt to dependence and of dependence to internal colonization, may make these abstractions more concrete.

Farmer Revolt and the First Revolution

As early as 1730, small farmers forced out of settled coastal areas into the wilder counties just east of the Appalachian Range were squatting on easterners' lands, refusing to pay rent to absentee landlords and withholding taxes from colonial assemblies. From Georgia to the New Hampshire Grants (Vermont) their grievances were listed, and they were always the same: they were underrepresented in the assemblies, threatened with loss of land through foreclosure and loss of freedom through seizure for debt, burdened with discriminatory taxes, prey to corrupt tax collectors and bribable court officials, unprotected against Indian attacks, and held in contempt by the eastern "aristocracy." Occasionally, the steady stream of complaints and petitions was punctuated by violence: in the 1730's revenue officials were tarred and feathered in South Carolina; in 1741 debtor farmers in western Massachusetts marched on Boston in support of a land bank law; and a few years later New Jerseyites refusing to pay their rents offered armed resistance to court officials sent to arrest them. It was not until the 1760's, however, that the revolt began to spread up and down the frontier.

In 1763 Britain concluded a treaty with France ending the Seven Years' War, and took title to all lands west of the colonies to the Mississippi, save Spanish Florida. Almost immediately there began an intensification of the twin pressures which were to generate two anticolonial revolts — that of the farmers and that of the patriots. Parliament enacted a series of harsh tax and trade measures, attempted to enforce others which had become dead letters, and cut off land speculation and settlement in the Ohio Valley, thus putting pressure on the large commercial and farming interests which controlled the eastern assemblies. Simultaneously, eastern interests began to "squeeze" the West for payment of rents and taxes, foreclosing and evicting debtors, challenging defective titles and buying up land. Unable to leave failing farms to "squat" on richer land across the mountains, ill-protected against the Indians (who united under Pontiac in 1763 to hold the line of settlement east of the Appalachians), and threatened by the prospect of peonage — for the alternative to debtors' prison was forced labor for creditors — the farmers turned increasingly to violence.

In 1763 the Paxton Boys, a group of frontiersmen from western Pennsylvania infuriated by the failure of the Quaker Assembly to protect them from Indian attack, revenged themselves on some helpless Christianized Indians and successfully resisted arrest. In 1764 they gathered a force of a thousand and marched on Philadelphia, but did not give battle when the Quakers armed for defense. Four years later western farmers in North Carolina, styling themselves "Regulators," gained control of the North Carolina Assembly; in the following year, the colony's governor dissolved the assembly and the Regulators took up arms.

They intimidated tax collectors into resigning their commissions, raided courthouses, and ran judges out of the territory to prevent them from foreclosing farms and indicting rebels. The colony's militia was called out in 1769, but as it proved thoroughly Regulator-infiltrated, the governor would not risk it in battle. Compromise legislation correcting some of the most obvious abuses was passed by the North Carolina legislature in 1770, but the insurgent leadership (repudiating the advice of moderate leaders like Assemblyman Herman Husbands) rejected the offer, raiding the Hillsboro courthouse in defiance. When the Regulators risked a massed battle with eastern militia at Allamance Creek in 1771, the battle turned into a rout, and their power — after three years of *de facto* control of the western counties — was broken.

Ending a revolt in one colony, however, did not necessarily deter rebels elsewhere. Before Massachusetts farmers fired the first shots of revolution, further uprisings took place in the New Hampshire Grants and in New Jersey. Moreover, the Revolution itself did not solve the problem of increasing farmer dependence on eastern moneyed interests (the North and South Carolina Regulators, foreseeing this, threw in their lot with the Tories during the actual fighting). In fact, the war was a catastrophe for veterans who, like Captain Daniel Shays of Massachusetts, returned home to find their land unplowed and their debts increased, commodity prices depressed and taxes at an all-time high, foreclosures increasing and the eastern legislatures (now state legislatures) as malapportioned and merchant-dominated as ever. The war had ended neither imprisonment for debt nor forced labor for creditors; it had not lowered court fees or abolished property qualifications for voting. In 1786 Massachusetts taxes were equal to one-third of the estimated income of her citizens, and Massachusetts was not unique. The result was two farmer uprisings of national importance: Shays' Rebellion and the Whiskey Rebellion.

In 1786 a small group of Massachusetts debtor farmers seized the Northampton courthouse, Regulator style, to prevent the court from sitting to foreclose mortgages and levy attachments for debt. Quickly organized, the violence spread, led by Captain Shays and other veterans of the war. Courthouses were seized and burned, government agents intimidated or roughed up, and the property of "collaborators" (as in Great Barrington) destroyed. In view of the military problems involved in sending a militia of doubtful loyalty to fight westerners on their home grounds, the Massachusetts General Assembly offered a compromise in 1787. It was rejected by Shays, whose program now included amnesty for insurgents, abolition of the upper house of the state legislature, legislative reapportionment and alterations in the manner of tax collection. Shortly thereafter Shays' seizure of the Worcester courthouse frightened eastern propertied men so badly that they offered to equip a punitive expedition at their own expense. Finally (in part because of a communications failure which deprived him of half his force), Shays' army of 1800 was defeated by General Benjamin Lincoln's 4400 before the arsenal at Springfield. The insurgents were dispersed, and several leaders captured and hanged. Shays escaped to New York and was granted a pardon as part of the general amnesty enacted in 1788.

Only a short time elapsed before a further revolt erupted, this time in Pennsylvania. In the interim, the Constitutional Convention in Philadelphia had hammered out the legal framework for a federal government; Captain Shays' rebellion and some economic experimentation by Rhode Island helped to persuade many delegates that strong central power was a necessity. The first military test of this power was provoked (some cynics say deliberately) by passage of Alexander Hamilton's ten cents per gallon excise tax on whiskey — a measure opposed by Jeffersonians in Congress and by some state legislatures. They felt that it discriminated against the poor (rye whiskey was currency in the West, the only form in which small farmers could market grain at a profit after the long haul east) to help the rich (tax receipts would fund the national debt, paying off government creditors at full value while currency depreciation pauperized the lower classes). Pennsylvania herself had a whiskey tax on the books which had never been enforced; but the big distillers viewed Hamilton's tax as a boon, since it would put the small fry out of business.

Between passage of the excise in 1791 and 1794, western farmers mobilized successfully to avoid payment. Their methods were familiar: tax collectors and process servers driven out of western counties, the homes of pro-government men burned or looted, and farmers attempting to pay the tax terrorized and intimidated. A repeal movement led by Jeffersonians in Congress was crushed; the new "democratic societies," local clubs friendly to Jefferson and French revolutionary ideals, became active among the farmers. In 1794, by way of compromise, Congress freed defendants in tax cases from the burden of traveling hundreds of miles to court in Philadelphia. Some ten thousand insurgents, including sympathizers from other states, responded by denouncing Congress at a mass meeting at Braddock's Field and then marching on Pittsburgh. The march was peaceful (its leaders well-known Jeffersonians like Albert Gallatin and H. H. Brackenridge), but it demonstrated to President Washington that the rebels were in control of large areas of the frontier and that contact had been established with disadvantaged farmers in New York, North Carolina, Virginia and the Ohio Valley.

At the time of Shays' Rebellion, George Washington had attempted to distinguish between justified and unjustified grievances. He reacted with similar caution to the Pennsylvania revolt — ordering the insurgents to disperse, but appointing a commission to investigate the causes of the disturbance and to make recommendations. Acting as presidential envoys, the commissioners offered the insurgents amnesty and forgiveness of past tax delinquency, provided the tax would be paid beginning in 1794 and formal submission made to federal authority. Rejecting the advice of the Gallatin leadership, more fiery leaders like David Bradford refused to follow the recommendations of the commission, and Washington himself finally led a parade of 12,000 troops into the western counties. There was no resistance; the revolt collapsed. Only two leaders were jailed, and the rest pardoned.

Except for brief flare-ups in South Carolina and again in Pennsylvania (1799), this was the last serious episode of farmer revolt on the Appalachian frontier. In 1800 Thomas Jefferson was elected President, and in the two decades afterwards, as state after state came under the sway of the Democratic-Republicans, property qualifications for suffrage were lowered or eliminated and legislatures reapportioned. Indian resistance to trans-Appalachian settlement was extinguished (more about this later); and as settlers poured into the area, they found themselves in control of their own states, from Kentucky and Tennessee to Ohio and Indiana. In 1803 the Louisiana Purchase opened the vast interior to settlement, and by 1828 the transformation was complete: western farmers in alliance with eastern workingmen and artisans put Andrew Jackson in the White House. The sons of North Carolina Regulators and Green Mountain Boys, Shays Rebels and Whiskey insurrectionists danced in their muddy boots at an inauguration ball.

The parallels between the western farmers' struggle against the eastern establishment and the patriots' fight against the British and Tories are striking. They illustrate the way in which colonization of domestic out-groups produces revolts aimed at establishing *de facto* independence on the rebels' home grounds. Like the westerners, the colonies had been left in relative peace for almost a century prior to passage of the Stamp Act. They were accustomed to exercising a great deal of control over their own local institutions, both political and economic, and viewed British attempts following the Peace of Paris to assert her sovereignty at the local level as usurpation. So long as they were left more or less alone, the colonists considered themselves Englishmen regardless of periodic squabbles over the royal governor's salary and the exercise of his veto. Again like the westerners, they exhausted their legal remedies before going against the law, and even then resorted first to civil disobedience and only afterwards to direct action. As the struggle escalated, however, they were exposed to further invasion on their home grounds and responded violently, discovering in the process their peoplehood.

The "Intolerable Acts," which led directly to Concord Bridge, were felt to be intolerable precisely because, by quartering troops in private houses, circumventing colonial juries in cases of political crime, closing the port of Boston and revoking the Massachusetts charter, they threatened the colonists with loss of control over their livelihoods, their town meetings and even the privacy of their homes. "Freedom," in the colonial lexicon, referred to a local and personal autonomy protected by certain orderly patterns of behavior taken for granted prior to 1765. In threatening to alter these patterns through aggressive colonialism, the British awakened in *all* classes of colonists the fear of political subjection and social chaos, and gave the revolutionary movement a powerful, educated leadership. The peculiarly conservative nature of the Revolution, which has been the subject of much historical study, is closely linked with its reactive or defensive nature; its aim, after all, was not to overthrow the British government but to restore a liberty which seemed to have been lost. Much the same thing may be said of the Appalachian farmer revolts, as well as of other American rebellions even to our own day.

The example of the Revolution illustrates also the close connection in the psychology of the domestic rebel between fear of dependence and fear of chaos. The Regulators, as their name suggests, were prototypal vigilantes, taking the law into their own hands because it had gotten out of their hands, seeking an order based on their own will because they had experienced the disorder of colonial subjection. To be dependent upon others, especially when the others represent an aggressive "civilizing" power, is to experience a high degree of social disorder — to witness the transformation of one's society by forces which seem arbitrary, capricious and uncontrollable. Personally, it is a degrading experience; indeed, the classical feudal definition of the serf — the lowest of the low — was that he did not perform fixed services for his lord but worked "at the lord's will." Therefore, the American rebel is often a vigilante; he seeks, through imposition of the group will on a chaotic, rapidly changing environment, to establish "law and order." But it is important to note that despite the conservative rhetoric of rebellion (the appeal to ancient rights, liberties and customs), the law and order which it proposes to create is a *new* law and order based upon a *new* group consciousness. Studies of American vigilantism which characterize the phenomenon as "reactionary violence," "native fascism," or "mob rule" make the mistake of taking rhetoric at face value. In fact, domestic revolts are very often both "radical" and "reactionary" in modern political terms since they hark back to lost (sometimes mythical) customs and liberties while attempting to create a new society. Eugene V. Debs — hardly a reactionary — never tired of pointing out that aggressive capitalists, not American workers, had changed the status quo.

Finally, both farmer revolt and patriot revolution demonstrate how benevolent colonialists react to the birth of violent independence movements: they offer compromises which are intended to remedy specific *grievances* without making fundamental changes in the colonial *relationship*. Typically such offers, no matter how well intended, are rejected as attempts to perpetuate the dependence of the colonized (they usually are), and the rejection further embitters and frustrates the authorities, inclining them to increased violence. We will explore this difficult dialogue in more detail in Chapter 5; its repetition could be costly and dangerous for America in the 1970's.

Southern Revolt and the "Second Revolution"

The coalition of South and West which brought Andrew Jackson to power contained a canker which would utterly destroy it within thirty years of its triumph. The canker was not Vice-President Calhoun (whom Jackson called a "base, unprincipled villain" and threatened to hang because of his role in the nullification controversy) but what Calhoun represented — the progressive alienation and unification of the white South. In 1830 the South Carolinians' bête noire was the high tariff which allegedly discriminated against southern agriculture in favor of northern industry; but South Carolina stood alone in her abortive attempt to "nullify" the federal law. By 1860, when South Carolinians fired on Fort Sumter, the tariff was a secondary issue and most white men south of the border states were united in their desire to secede rather than accept Abraham Lincoln as president. What caused Virginia gentlemen and Georgia crackers, Louisiana cotton kings and Alabama dirt farmers to forget their differences and act as one? Why did they do so in 1860? The answer lies, in part, in the connection between increasing dependence and group violence.

As W. J. Cash and others have pointed out, there was little difference, except in cash value, between those rough and ready frontier businessmen who made fortunes in cotton, sugar, indigo or slave breeding and those who missed out. The old "aristocracy" — the planters who had dominated the Old South at the time of the farmer revolts — had fallen on evil times. With tobacco farming no longer profitable, they were compelled to export their only crop of value — slaves needed in the cotton, indigo and rice plantations of the New South. For the new aristocracy — those who had been able to unite enough good land with enough slaves to make the plantation system work — there was little security and less leisure. They lived in disaster's shadow, exposed to unpredictable fluctuations in the world price of agricultural exports, the constant need for new land to replace that burned out by voracious crops, and the presence of a restless, seething, ever multiplying class of slaves. By 1860, fearful of slave revolt and new John Browns, southerners had organized miniature armies which operated under police state regulations to keep the blacks in check.

57

The soldiers in these plantation armies and community patrols were small farmers, agricultural laborers and the unemployed — the "yeomen" who Jefferson had thought were the last, best hope of the Republic. Westward expansion, which added to the industrial strength of the North the incomparable farmland of the Midwest and plains states, had brought the South little of comparable value. Moreover, so far as farming was concerned, there was no labor cheaper in the short run than slave labor, and most southern whites would not soil their hands with "nigger work" — which included much of the early industrial and craft labor performed in the North by white artisans. Therefore, the southern farmer's world was shrinking: he could become an overseer or guard on a plantation, or scratch the unproductive soil left over after the plantation owner had moved on. Or he could head west in search of land of his own, with the dream of a cotton and slave kingdom constantly before him. For him, as for the "aristocrat," the price of economic failure was social degradation. To be a loser in the antebellum South was to become the next best thing to a slave — it was to become that contradiction of contradictions, a tenant farmer, an American peasant.

Thus, internal pressures drove southern white men, rich and poor, closer together. In common, they feared the Negro yet wanted his service, craved new territory yet yearned for roots and social stability. In common, they lived on the edge of an economic-social precipice and, increasingly, they tended to blame failure in this harsh world on a common enemy. In this same period, the North was becoming an aggressive industrial nation. Its population, augmented by the great rush of European immigration, was booming; its agriculture was diversified and commercial; it was industrializing, building canals and railroads; its culture, arts and letters were flourishing as never before. None of these statements could be made of the South, where slave labor discouraged immigration and the one-crop system stultified agriculture, where industry was virtually nonexistent and "southern culture" a frontier myth. While the North was becoming a nation, the white South became an ethnic group. It was in imminent danger of lapsing, economically and politically, into a state of utter dependence on the modernizing Yankees.

The threat of increasing dependence helps to explain a psychological puzzle which has often troubled historians: the strange disparity between southern fear and southern power. As Samuel Eliot Morison put it, in connection with southern threats to secede in 1850:

It is difficult to grasp the real reason for all this sound and fury. After all, as Henry Clay pointed out, the Southern States had an equal vote in the Senate, a majority in the cabinet and the Supreme Court, and a President who was Virginia-born and Louisiana bred. Since 1801 the South had obtained from the Union all that she really wanted — free trade . . . protection to slavery in the national capital, vast theaters for slavery extension such as Louisiana, Florida, the Indian Territory and Texas. Only extreme abolitionists threatened to interfere with slavery where it presently existed. . . .

Probably we need a psychotherapist to analyze the complexes of that day. . . .[1]

This paranoia, if such it was, was even more pronounced a decade later. Under President Buchanan, the South had a near monopoly of important federal offices, southerners dominated the officer corps of the United States Army and the only hostile act that could reasonably be expected from the nonabolitionist Lincoln (in the unlikely event of his election) was the prohibition of slavery in certain new territories. Yet in the summer of 1860 the South bolted the Democratic party, destroying Stephen Douglas's chances of becoming President and *insuring* the election of Lincoln. Then, with Lincoln elected, the southern states seceded in protest of his election! To call this behavior pathological, of course, is to suggest that southern fears were exaggerated, or totally unfounded. But this, clearly, was not the case.

Long before 1860, perceptive southerners like Calhoun saw themselves doomed by the harsh facts of economics and politics to play the role of children dependent on the northern parent. To avert this fate, Calhoun had constructed his ingenious political and constitutional theories, which were intended to build southern power into the Constitution, or, in the alternative, to furnish a rationale for secession. The experiment was a failure, conceptually as well as politically, for in the last analysis, if the South were to remain underdeveloped relative to the North, nothing could save it from exercising national power at the North's sufferance. This may be why southerners reacted hysterically in the decade before the Civil War to events which did not really threaten them directly: the admission of California as a free state, abolitionist agitation in the North, northern immigration into Kansas and John Brown's abortive raid on Harpers Ferry. In effect, southern power was an illusion. The concessions which her senators had wrung from the North in a series of prewar compromises had not been based on the realities of power but extorted by threats to secede; moreover, each compromise represented a further shift of the decision-making power with respect to slavery and states' rights to a representative rather than a constitutional majority. In other words, although the southern bloc could exercise a veto over threatening constitutional amendments, that power became meaningless if questions of slavery and states' rights were to be decided in any other forum — in Congress, for example, or in the territories themselves. For this reason Stephen Douglas's theory of "popular sovereignty" embodied in the Kansas-Nebraska Act of 1854, which put the slave or free status of future states up to their settlers, proved to be the last of the "great compromises" and drove the South to oppose Douglas in 1860.

Looked at from a modern perspective, the southern dilemma is familiar enough: how to generate in an essentially backward, agrarian society the kind of economic strength, political power and psychic pride which will enable its members to avoid becoming the serfs of the modern industrial state. It is a problem with which modern agricultural nations wrestle daily, and which they have attempted to solve (usually unsuccessfully) by a variety of methods including forced industrialization, collectivization of agriculture, and special favors such as subsidization, malapportionment of legislatures and agricultural tariffs. The southern solution was slavery, which combined with the plantation system of farming to produce (so the southerners thought) both a viable, commercial agriculture — the rough nineteenth-century equivalent of collectivization — and the social basis for a separate, "higher" culture and civilization. The only protection for this expansive system was the South's constitutional veto, whose efficacy in fact depended on the willingness of Congress to permit its exercise. This willingness, in turn, was supported by political divisions in the North between and within the major parties. The first protective factor was eliminated by the Kansas-Nebraska Act and the second by the rise of the Republican party and the election of Lincoln.

For psychological as well as strategic reasons, groups confronted with the prospect of increasing dependence on powerful outsiders sometimes react by taking the offensive. If successful, they may succeed in replacing dependence with "independence"; but even if they fail, the shame of complicity in a degrading relationship is washed away. No stigma attaches to involuntary dependence; conquest and occupation may even create a sustaining hope of future greatness. The South went on the offensive in 1854, after Congress passed the Kansas-Nebraska Act. As her leaders realized, "popular sovereignty" implicitly favored the more populous section. It spelled the end of southern equality in the Senate, and, more important, established on a local level the principle of majoritarian authority over the slavery question. Henceforth, the South's only protection would reside in *the willingness of the majority to avoid oppressing her*. Not surprisingly, Kansas-Nebraska became the scene of a little civil war, with both sides contributing settlers and arms; and, still not surprisingly, the North won. Those in each section with the highest stake in the outcome were the poorer classes, for both northern wage earners and southern farmers saw the Great Plains as a last resort — the field on which their dreams might one day be realized if all else failed. That their visions of success had become incompatible helps to explain the breakup of the nation four years later.

The South lost the Kansas war; Kansas and Nebraska were admitted as free territory before the Civil War began. Nevertheless, southerners continued to press their kamikaze offensive to its inevitable conclusion, calling for implementation of the Dred Scott decision (1856, holding slavery to be incapable of abolition even in free states!), reopening of the slave trade, conquest of more slave territory in Latin America, and finally, control of the national

Democratic party. When the national Democratic convention of 1860 rejected an extreme proslavery platform, the southern delegates walked out, with predictable results: John Cabell Breckinridge was nominated as a southern third-party candidate, the split vote cost Stephen Douglas the election, and the South seceded. There was an air of symbolic formality about all of this; having slapped the North's face as honor required, southerners went to war as to a duel. South Carolina was given the "privilege" of making the initial attack on Fort Sumter, and the war commenced — not with guerrilla attacks, sabotage, or assassination, but with picture-book battles observed at safe distances by ladies and gentlemen with opera glasses. And so it continued, with the gallant Lee declining to attack Washington or to resort to guerrilla warfare — until a technician, Grant, ended it at Richmond. Yet even Grant permitted the insurgents to keep their weapons after the surrender — an act of generosity which boomeranged two years later when terrorists began to use them against Negroes and occupying troops.

What the Civil War decided was the issue of southern independence, and that it decided unambiguously. The war's end found the South a shambles — socially disordered, economically prostrate and politically powerless. There was now no question either of the Union's disintegrating or of the South's maintaining its specially protected status as a shield against northern power. Ambiguities, however, remained. Less than two years after Appomattox another war began on southern soil — this time a guerrilla struggle rather than a formal war — and the issue was again, but in a new sense, independence.

The rise of the Ku Klux Klan and other terrorist groups after 1867 poses a critical comparative question: why would southerners, already thoroughly defeated in the most costly war in the nation's history, rise again to battle while other oppressed out-groups (for example, western farmers of the 1870's and 1880's) pursued their aims non-violently? After all, the state of affairs which we have characterized as "the southern dilemma" — the increasing dependence of an agrarian society on an industrial society modernizing at a more rapid rate — was also characteristic of the farmers of the West and South throughout the nineteenth and well into the twentieth centuries. Nevertheless, unlike the southern power movement, the farmer power movement (whether called Greenback, Granger, Farmers' Alliance, Populist or Farmer-Labor) resorted rarely to mass violence, and never to organized guerrilla warfare. Analysis of the comparison may tell us something more about the nature of domestic political violence.

Quasi

*I*n the Civil War, white southerners fought to obtain their maximum group demand — juridical independence — and lost. After 1867, they fought to obtain their minimum demand — local autonomy on southern soil — and won. The precipitants of this struggle — a familiar succession of events — consisted of great group success followed by a shocking reversal. Although slavery had been abolished, between 1865 and 1867 it seemed certain that the benign policies of Lincoln and Johnson would permit restoration in substance of the "southern way of life." In 1867, however, Radical Republicans in Congress gained the votes necessary to pass their own reconstruction plans over the President's veto. Congress never went as far in attempting to reconstruct the South as the more extreme radicals would have liked; men like Wendell Phillips foresaw in its refusal to break up large landed estates the inevitable reduction of southern Negroes to economic serfdom.

4.

Independence and Local Power

Nevertheless, it went far enough, by passing civil rights acts, amending the Constitution, disenfranchising ex-Confederates, protecting Negro political organizations and supervising elections with troops, to create sufficient southern support for another independence — or rather quasi-independence — revolt.

What the white South sought was clearly not legal independence but its functional equivalent: white control over local political institutions, economic opportunities and social customs and mores. This translated, of course, into total domination of blacks and white Republicans, who by coalescing were threatening to transform southern society. Thus, throughout the late 1860's, rumors of impending massacres and reports of rapes of white women — the paranoiac harbingers of genuine social change — abounded. Some black men, coming home from meetings of the Union League, were no longer willing to step into the street to let white men go by on the sidewalk; others spoke disrespectfully to their former masters. White "scalawags" addressed black political gatherings with dangerous fervor, and a few even lived openly with Negro women! Everything seemed topsy-turvy, especially with Negroes and northern emigrants sitting in state legislatures. That these legislatures were no more corrupt than their counterparts in the North and, in fact, enacted a great deal of pioneering social legislation was irrelevant to men who considered them alien oppressors.

White southerners were thus held together by a common hatred of "alien" government, a common fear of competition from free black labor, and a common conviction that the social order was disintegrating. Under these conditions the Ku Klux Klan, started as a harmless fraternal order in Pulaski, Tennessee, was soon welded by former Confederate general Nathan Bedford Forrest into a cooperative coalition of guerrilla bands. The Knights of the White Camellia arose in Louisiana; in South Carolina, interestingly enough, the terrorists called themselves Regulators. All such organizations, composed principally of Confederate veterans, were organized on military-fraternal lines, with a heavy emphasis on secrecy, passwords, oaths and rituals. Their purpose was, by intimidating Negroes, agents of carpetbag governments and "unpatriotic" southerners, to return control of all local government functions to white supremacists, and to reestablish in substance the system of social norms and folkways that had existed before the war.

It would be foolish, however, to take the reactionary rhetoric of white "redemption" at face value. What was being established by force was, in fact, a *new* order, in which, for example, blacks would be ousted from the industrial or craft jobs they had held before the war, and this formerly despised "nigger work" turned over to whites seeking employment. Indeed, the ideology of redemption went beyond mere racism to a sort of southern Zionism in which the values of work, self-government, militant self-defense and communal regeneration were rediscovered. With this ideological underpinning, using classical guerrilla hit and run techniques and supported by a probable majority of the white population, the rebels were entirely successful. Blacks were frightened or beaten into staying away from the polls, dissolving their political organizations, and returning to passive subservience. Carpetbaggers who strayed away from state capitals into the countryside were driven out of state, beaten, or, in some cases, assassinated. The machinery of Reconstruction government was disrupted by sabotage; and those white southerners who had thought about giving their allegiance to the Republican coalition thought again, and declared it illegitimate. In a pattern which has since become familiar, those who dared violate traditional social taboos were hounded out of the South.

In a few cases, Reconstructionists in power fought back with some success, but even in Arkansas, where severe military reprisals were taken against the Klan, the result was merely an armed truce. By the time the Grant administration began to take an interest in terrorist activities, the Reconstruction governments were being isolated, militarily, politically and spiritually, from the white population. In the North there was little interest in Klan activity until the congressional hearings of 1870–1871, and by the time Congress enacted strong legislation against terrorist organizations, it was too late. With blacks staying away from the polls and whites becoming reenfranchised, the "carpetbag" governments fell like leaves. General Forrest and his fellow aristocrats apparently feared losing control of the Klan's operations to unorganized poor whites; they or-

69

dered its dissolution, and its activities declined. By 1876, when Rutherford Hayes triumphed over Samuel Tilden in a disputed election, promising as part of the deal which gave him the presidency to remove the remaining federal troops from the South, there were only three states still militarily occupied. The second war of southern independence was over.

Several aspects of the revolt are of particular interest in the light of subsequent historical developments. By supporting K.K.K. activity both passively and actively, white southerners told the North, in effect: "We will accept military defeat, legal union, even economic and political dependence upon the more powerful section; but we will *not* accept military occupation, rule by outsiders or a managed social transformation *on our own home grounds.*" In a sense, the Civil War had been a preemptive attack. Despite failure of this tactic at a terrible cost to both sides, it seemed that the guerrilla fight to rid the South of "alien rule" could continue indefinitely. The North's acquiescence in Klan terror and white supremacist redemption, although often attributed to war weariness, racial prejudice, etc., was at bottom based on recognition that the suppression of a popular guerrilla war would be costly indeed. (Republicans like Carl Schurz, unwilling to suspend civil liberties indefinitely in the South, opposed Grant's Force Act of 1871.) Of course, this decision condemned both blacks and southern dissenters to a century of totalitarian rule. Between 1880 and 1900 the violence of 1867–1876 became institutionalized; there were in these years more than two thousand *reported* lynchings of whites and blacks. Nevertheless, in 1865 there were only two feasible alternatives open to the North: either acceptance and enforcement of the extreme Radicals' program, which would have necessitated destruction of the southern landed aristocracy; or acquiescence in the demand for quasi-independence. From the perspective of the 1960's the first alternative seems preferable (Cuba and North Vietnam, for example, permitted their landowners to go into exile after expropriation), but the second was finally adopted.

Unfortunately, it is customary to treat southern terrorism, whether insurrectionary or institutionalized, as *sui generis* — a uniquely southern reaction to a unique racial problem. Liberal historians and social scientists have been only too happy to pin the impulse toward violence on the reactionary South, either ignoring "radical" violence or distinguishing it from "racist terrorism." From the viewpoint of the late 1960's, however, the artificiality of such distinctions is apparent. We can see, for example, that "radical" labor violence was very often directed downward against blacks, Orientals and newer immigrants; and that the black nationalism of the 1960's is startlingly similar in some respects to the "reactionary" southern nationalism of the 1860's. I refer, of course, not to the direction of violence socially downward, since modern blacks remain at the bottom of the socioeconomic ladder, but to the desire of both groups to establish, by force if necessary, their collective autonomy on the home ground. The urge of outgroups toward quasi-independence — the maximum degree of local autonomy consistent with membership in a legally unified nation — lies close to the heart of both revolts.

Later we discuss the black revolt of 1964–1968 in some detail. It seems fairly clear, however, that for many urban blacks white storekeepers, landlords and policemen working in the ghetto are the functional equivalent of the carpetbaggers and federal troops of 1867–1876, and conservative leaders like Ralph Bunche and Roy Wilkins the "scalawags." In both cases the claim to control territory is bolstered by nationalistic fervor — group pride arising from the ashes of humiliation. In both cases, rebel leaders aim to replace "alien" and therefore illegitimate institutions of local government with institutions more representative of an oppressed constituency. In both cases, group nationalism stresses the possibility of collective redemption through self-help, the value of work and self-discipline and the need to draw economic and moral strength from within the group rather than from without.

Of course, there were significant differences between the two revolts. White southerners had an underclass to oppress, and, having already experienced a military independence struggle, were prepared to back their old leaders in an organized campaign of terror and retribution. In 1969, urban blacks were only beginning their struggle. Revolutionaries did not yet command the support of the masses, whose political consciousness and loyalties were in flux. "Black power" described an inconsistent set of ideologies ranging from "black capitalism" to visionary socialism. The violence which emerged in the 1960's was therefore for the most part unplanned, unorganized and unled. But it was in the tradition of independence revolt. At the end of the period 1964–1968 there were a great many blacks (one poll estimated their number at two million) favoring the establishment of an independent black nation located somewhere within the present boundaries of the United States. Others, probably more numerous by far, favored the maximum independence possible within the existing legal system — for example, local control of inner-city governments, police departments, economic enterprises and educational institutions.

As should be clear from our earlier discussion of rebellious domestic groups, however, the desire of the internally colonized for quasi-independence or local autonomy has by no means been limited to white southerners and black northerners. Indeed, it seems to be the clearest single thread running through revolts as diverse as those of the Appalachian farmers and southeastern Indians, Philadelphia nativists and New York Irish. And for good reason. The control of local territory was, traditionally, the most effective way to break the cycle of weakness and more weakness, dependence and more dependence which characterized groups modernizing too slowly to force an entry into the power structure. Like infant industries protected by tariff walls, American groups sometimes developed behind ghetto walls the power, pride and inventiveness needed to compete with more powerful outsiders. And even where this did not occur, group power on the local level sometimes compensated, psychologically, for powerlessness nationally. In modern terms, it prevented, or at least reduced, group alienation.

To illustrate, consider the significance of local autonomy for so-called "nonviolent" out-groups — for example, western farmers between the Civil War and the New Deal. "Nonviolent," of course, is a relative term; in addition to "wild West" carnage in the form of Indian wars, frontier vigilantism, range wars and family feuds, organized debtor farmers after the Civil War sometimes resorted to Regulator style action in hard times. (The last major outbreak of this kind was the Farmers' Holiday Association violence of the early 1930's, in which farmers ruined by the Depression fought to keep their homesteads out of the hands of court officials and bankers; but even as recently as 1966, members of the National Farmers' Organization were pouring milk on the highways and threatening to burn grain.) Turbulence in farming areas is an old story in America. Still, one cannot help but notice the difference between the farmer power movement and more violent re-

volts in American history. By contrast with white southerners or modern blacks, the farmers of 1870–1930 seem
tame indeed.

From the close of the Civil War until Roosevelt's second
administration the energies which debtor farmers might
have poured into insurrections or nightriding were devoted
principally to electoral politics. Movements proliferated,
each offering a new prescription for the ills of the countryside and the subordination of agrarian to industrial power:
funny money, free silver, cooperatives, the nationalization
of industry, prohibition. Between 1870 and 1890, Populists dedicated to increasing farmer power through currency inflation and government control of farm-related industries swept into power in state after state. Combining
bloodcurdling rhetoric with grassroots political organization, they built a West-South axis whose votes in Congress
helped to pass the Interstate Commerce and Sherman
Antitrust acts. Populists nominated James B. Weaver for
President in 1892, and supported William Jennings Bryan
in his three tries for the White House. As Richard Hofstadter put it, "Bryan's typical constituent was the long-
suffering staple farmer of the West and South" whose
"long-term debts were appreciating intolerably" between
1865 and 1895, and who was "victimized by tariffs, middlemen, speculators, warehousers and monopolistic producers of farm equipment." [1] Yet, despite this continuing
victimization, and despite Bryan's habit of losing elections,
the movement remained essentially nonviolent.

Why? The decade of farm prosperity prior to the First
World War helped, of course, but even in severe depres-
sions like those of 1877, 1893 and 1929, when workingmen fought bloody strikes with company armies, there was
comparative peace on the farm. The answer, I think, is
implicit in the *local* successes of the Populists. Farmers did

not have to resort to violence to achieve quasi-independence because they had already won it. If their political revolt was a dismal failure nationally, it was nevertheless true that, on the state and local level, staple producers had succeeded in electing governments which would represent their interests against those of the railroads, bankers and middlemen. (It will be recalled that Populist legislatures in the 1870's and 1880's pioneered in attempting to regulate big business.) Organizations like the Grange and the Farmers' Alliances, however weak in Washington (and they were not entirely impotent), satisfied the need for militant political representation — for leaders considered "legitimate" both by the group and by the legal system. Even more important, perhaps, strong social organization brought with it a sense of communal solidarity and social control; it protected farmers against the terror of rapid change in social customs, mores and habits of life. Finally, in the same years that strong local political and social organizations were developing, economic experimentation could and did take place, with farmers adopting institutional innovations like producers' cooperatives along with technological innovations like McCormick's reaper.

To be sure, the feeling of collective autonomy generated by local organization was, in a sense, illusory, since the level of commodity prices could hardly be controlled by state legislatures or Granges. But (by definition, really) the existence of group pride, solidarity and a sense of independence meant the absence of "alienation." With farmer power a reality, at least locally, there was little of that naked exploitation or overt rule by outsiders which so infuriated out-groups like Reconstruction southerners and modern ghetto blacks. The farmers may have been oppressed, but at least on the home ground they were not entirely defenseless.

This suggests a further relationship between the resort to violence and the out-group's inability to achieve quasi-independence on its home ground. To put it abstractly, it appears that political and social control of local institutions has sometimes served, or promised to serve, as a brake upon the increasing dependence of colonized groups. A case in point is the use of local autonomy and white solidarity by southerners to defeat northern attempts to alter the nature of that society. Another is the effort by various black self-defense organizations to "police the police" on ghetto streets and ultimately to achieve a transfer of the policing function to representatives of black communities. On the other hand, local autonomy may only disguise increasing dependence, or make it more palatable. This occurs when centralizing forces are very strong and central power can be exercised at a distance, without the necessity for interference on the out-group's territory. In such cases (for example, twentieth-century farmers, industrial workers and minority groups), quasi-independence is not enough; the out-group can hold its own only by combining local power with strong influence at the center. However, whether quasi-independence proves to be effective or illusory, one thing is clear: groups lacking it will fight for it even where their oppression is relatively light; and groups possessing it will tend to keep the peace even where their oppression is severe.

This helps us to understand better why there has been so much *insurrectionary* violence and so little *revolutionary* violence in America. Internal colonization awakens in colonized groups a sense of cultural and political identity, and the presence of outsiders on group territory presents a clear challenge to group pride, as well as a tempting target for self-defensive violence. If the outsiders cannot be banished by means of peaceful political activity or economic

pressure, they will be driven out by force. In a heterogene-
ous, economically mobile, constantly centralizing nation
like the United States, the process of colonization, group
awakening and confrontation occurs with increasing fre-
quency, and as territory which can be claimed and held
disappears (especially in the urban setting), mass violence
born of desperation becomes more common. Note, however, that when quasi-independence is achieved, especially
where it is ineffective to reverse the trend toward increasing dependence, those still unhappy with their status must
decide either to play the game of coalition politics or to
attempt to foment a revolution — to seize power by force
at the center. For a variety of reasons, most quasi-
independent groups, like the farmers, have adopted the
first alternative. Quasi-independence itself removes visible
outrages upon the local population, and eliminates easy
targets; after its achievement, group members wishing to
persist in violence must invade the outsiders' territory. (It
has been very hard in America, despite the most severe
oppression, to mobilize group sentiment for such an "aggressive" war.) Moreover, the very solidarity which helps
to achieve local power stands in the way of more revolutionary activity by the poor; group consciousness, as it
were, weakens class consciousness, and the leadership of
the quasi-independent group is likely to be middle-class, or
at least antirevolutionary. (This is as true of most black
power leaders as it was of Populist leaders.) Most important, there *has* been a causal connection between local
autonomy and success in gaining power at the center.
Groups which have been able to combine militant demands for change with the ability to control votes have
improved their chances of gaining entry into the political
party system.

The critical importance of local autonomy in the urban

setting is illustrated by comparing the rise to power of urban immigrant groups like the Irish, Italians, Poles and Jews with that of the labor movement. (Although many labor unionists were immigrants, the comparison is still instructive.) Focusing on urban ethnic groups to begin with, one perceives immediately the strong connection between violence and territory. Battles between street gangs, warfare between organized criminal organizations, nativist and race rioting and sporadic terrorism (threats, bombings, arson, etc.) were usually directed against outsiders attempting to infiltrate territory claimed by another group. In considering this type of urban violence, some social scientists have misleadingly focused on the purely irrational or symbolic aspects of territoriality, forgetting that maintaining control over a defined geographic area was also a method of maximizing real power. In instances of what Morris Janowitz calls "communal violence," groups possessing a high degree of economic and ethnic coherence defended not just their "turf" but their control over the political machinery, educational and religious institutions, job opportunities and social mores (or tone) of the locality against invasion by newcomers.[2] This is the exception to the rule that groups possessing quasi-independence will not resort to further violence. They will almost inevitably resort to violence if that autonomy is threatened by overt invasion of their territory.

But in what respect is the other well-known type of urban disorder, which Janowitz calls "commodity" and William Kornhauser "antiauthority" violence, essentially different? Janowitz points out that the targets of the ghetto riots of the 1960's, for example, were not members of the white group *per se,* but property owned by whites and persons representing white authority, such as policemen and firemen.[3] Like the behavior of the Irish during the New

York draft riot of 1863, this behavior seems more "revolutionary" and less like "civil war" than, say, the Chicago race riot of 1919. But these terms are misleading; the differences between the two types of violence are of degree rather than of kind. Communal riots are territorial struggles between less and more dependent groups; antiauthority riots may be defined in the same way, except that the distance between the contestants on the sociopolitical scale is much greater. In the latter case, the struggle takes place when a group just awakening to its political identity and the possibility of local autonomy is confronted on local territory by the representatives of groups so strong that they can afford to exercise power through delegates, and at a distance. The local "authorities" attacked in "antiauthority" riots are attacked precisely because they are the servants of absentee proprietors who control the machinery of the law. Those defending the status quo may choose to characterize such conflicts as "the rebels vs. the law," but the rioters know better: they know it is not the law which they burn, loot and stone but those who manipulate it.

In the 1863 riot in New York City, for example, the violence of the Irish rioters was both "communal" and "antiauthority," since the same mobs sacked and burned federal draft offices and arsenals, killed firemen and policemen (including the chief of police), looted local stores and lynched Negroes in the black section of town. These actions were perfectly consistent, since the same authorities (generally WASPs, whether Republican or Democrat) were responsible both for conscripting the poor to fight in the South and encouraging the use of low-wage labor to break strikes on the New York waterfront. In fact, in many cases of labor violence — to which we shall now turn — one notices the coincidence of "communal" and "antiau-

79

thority" types. For example, during the wave of riots which swept the nation after the railroad strikes of 1877, San Francisco workingmen viciously attacked the Chinese community of that city (and several years later, AFL chief Samuel Gompers lobbied successfully on behalf of the Chinese Exclusion Act). Transcending this academic distinction, then, one perceives that labor violence, like other instances of group violence discussed herein, has generally been insurrectionary rather than revolutionary, directed not so much toward destroying the capitalist system as toward achieving of control over the immediate environment. For labor, the economic equivalent of territory is the job.

There has been a great deal of discussion about why American workingmen did not develop "class consciousness" as British and French workingmen did, why the American labor movement did not evolve into a labor party, and why the New Deal did not turn out to be a socialist revolution. These are interesting questions, but the way in which they are customarily asked, and answered, focuses attention on a contrast drawn from European experience which, at least until the 1930's, was irrelevant to America: the violent Marxist or anarcho-syndicalist organization vs. the peaceful trade union. Labor organizations in the United States have run the ideological gamut, but it is doubtful whether, in practice, Emma Goldman's anarchists or Eugene Debs's Wobblies were any more or less violent than the United Mine Workers of the 1920's, the AFL of the 1890's, or, for that matter, the unorganized railroad workers of the 1870's. From the terrorism of the Molly Maguires through the sit-down strikes in Detroit, American industrial workers of numerous ideological bents and diverse organizational affiliations fought violently against management and its allies. Labor historians Philip Taft and Philip Ross have pointed out that in sheer quantity of lives lost, personal injuries, and property damage, United States labor warfare exceeds that experienced by any other industrialized nation.[4] Therefore, it is not the contrast between revolutionary and peaceful organizations which concerns us but the nature of the turbulence, which was neither revolutionary nor insignificant. Indeed, it is so much a part of our national tradition that a certain amount of personal violence and sabotage during hard-fought strikes is now accepted as part of the game.

Notwithstanding the many works on "the rise of the modern labor union" it is important to remember that during most of the nineteenth and twentieth centuries it was not labor which was rising but capital. Even before the Civil War, American businessmen had begun to throw off traditional legal and moral inhibitions to business expansion, replacing special incorporation with general incorporation legislation, buying up state legislatures, and establishing the principle of one-way laissez-faire (government aid to business without government regulation). After the war, in the incredible scramble for concessions, franchises, public lands and legislative seats described by Mark Twain in *The Gilded Age,*[5] the cash market in political power ripened and was harvested. As a result, business could purchase the neutrality of government when it so desired; or, when outgunned by labor on a local level, it could call in federal troops. With their political hegemony thus assured, American capitalists proceeded to improvise a startling array of new institutions, from commodities exchanges to chambers of commerce, and from vertically integrated trusts to philanthropic foundations. Measured against this standard of increasing power and creativity, the labor movement in the same period seems almost pathetically retrograde and disorganized. Several distinctions make the contrast clear.

(1) The business class, pervaded by WASPs and "rugged individualists" who had separated themselves from their groups of origin, rose above ethnic and political differences to class consciousness; its capacity for cooperative action in the face of danger from the "common enemy" was proven again and again. The working class, riven by competing ethnic and racial loyalties, was rarely capable of concerted action on a national scale.

(2) Partly as a result of the above, and despite the efforts of Debs, Haywood, De Leon and other socialists, the principle of organization along craft lines dominated the American labor movement well into the 1930's. Industry, which had relegated craft organization of management to the dustbin after the Civil War, therefore enjoyed an immense advantage over labor in taking concerted action, bargaining and keeping control of basic economic decisions.

(3) As time went by, competition among capitalists was reduced by industrial concentration; but with new immigrants pouring into the United States in unprecedented waves, the temptation for workers to get and hold skilled or semiskilled jobs against the invaders, and to maintain ethnic group domination over certain crafts, was overwhelming. Much of labor's energy (and much violence) was therefore aimed at excluding the unskilled workers threatening from beneath rather than attempting to seize control of industry at the top.

(4) While business organization was rendered secure by the purchase of governmental favor, labor organization was rarely translated into control of city, country or state governments. Lacking local power bases, labor could not

enter into meaningful bargaining in the context of coalition politics, and did not gain a major voice in either national political party until the New Deal.

As a result of these comparative deficiencies, labor organizations operated for the most part on the economic level — at the job site only, so to speak. Their fortunes fluctuated with the business cycle, and in hard times, when layoffs and wage cuts threatened the livelihood of every workingman, they tended to come apart at the seams. Since hard times were violent times for both labor and management, it is important to note this correlation between increased labor violence and increasing disorganization. During periods of relative prosperity, or at the beginning of an economic downturn, workers in a particular craft or industry might organize in order to secure their jobs from competitive wage bidding and to gain a larger share of the pie. Often (as in the case of Debs's American Railway Union prior to the Pullman strike) newly organized workers won their initial strikes or (as in the case of the Steelworkers' Union prior to the Carnegie strike) achieved union recognition. When depression deepened, however, it was customary for large corporations to offset declining profits against wages rather than against either undistributed profits or dividends, and to withdraw recognition from unions which insisted upon maintaining wage standards and working conditions. Mass labor violence in transportation and manufacturing occurred frequently under these circumstances, since the combination of declining wage levels and collapsing organization threatened individual workers with pitiless exposure to wage competition. To put it another way, workers fought when the alternative was absolute insecurity and individual dependence upon management. It was no wonder that their principal targets were the unorganized, unskilled strikebreakers who threatened to take their jobs, the only valuable "property" labor possessed.

After Samuel Gompers made collective bargaining and job security through craft organization the basic philosophy of the AFL, thus breaking with the socialists who stood for political organization of the working class on an industrial basis, it became fashionable to speak of American labor's focus on wages, working conditions and the job as a philosophy differentiating the conservative American from the radical European labor movements. From the 1890's onward there was, to be sure, intense debate over ideology, strategy and tactics, not just between Gompers and the socialists, but between the left and right wings of each persuasion (and often between left and right wings of these wings!) Nevertheless, *in practice,* concentration on conditions at the job site and on the job itself was characteristic of the entire movement. This was not because Gompers's principles were universally accepted, but because, before proceeding to make a virtue of necessity, they accurately reflected the realities of economic power in the United States. It was labor rather than management that was up against the wall, fighting for survival; whether the leader was Gompers, Hilquist, Debs or William Z. Foster, industrial workers struck and fought to preserve a bare minimum of control over their lives and livelihood. With the exception of William D. Haywood's Western Federation of Miners (which we will discuss in a moment), there was little correlation between degree of ideological radicalism and willingness to resort to violence either under strike or nonstrike conditions. For example, the strikes of 1919, led in some cases by extreme radicals, were much less violent than those of 1877, in which unorganized railroad workers struck and then rioted in a dozen cities. Similarly, while anarcho-syndicalists called for, and in some cases practiced, sabotage and assassination, the undisputed "dynamite kings" of the early 1900's were AFL organizers, while as for assassination, no subsequent organization approached the ruthlessness of the old Molly Maguires.

We may therefore draw at least one parallel between industrial labor violence and other manifestations of political violence: workers, like members of other oppressed and excluded domestic groups, resorted to violence in order to forestall a slide into unlimited individual dependence upon powerful masters. They fought to preserve their collective existence against individualistic chaos, and their "territory" — their jobs — against invasion by outsiders. (And, in addition, they sometimes fought to prevent the lowering of wages below the subsistence level — a battle for life itself.) Following the now familiar pattern, workers ordinarily did not attack capitalists in person, but limited themselves to self-defensive actions against management agents (scabs and the private armies sent to protect them) and to the destruction of property. In most industries class warfare did *not* take the form of sustained revolt or insurrection on the model of the Klan uprisings or the modern ghetto revolts. It would be more accurate to describe the overall pattern from 1877 to 1937 as prolonged turbulence, sporadic and decentralized, with occasional outbursts of large-scale strike violence and terrorism. In certain industries — most notably mining and timber — labor violence approached or equaled other insurrectionary outbreaks in scope, duration and intensity; yet, even here, the outcome was inconclusive until the New Deal reorganized American labor relations and violence in all industries declined. The questions which thus plague the analyst are numerous and difficult: Why did the violence last so long? Why was it sporadic and disorganized? Why were the timber and extractive industries exceptionally violent? And what sort of "solution" to the problem did the New Deal represent?

To answer these questions, however tentatively, we must return to our theme: the significance of local power or "quasi-independence." As has been noted in a slightly different context, labor organizations lacked two characteristics possessed by other out-groups discussed herein — ethnic cohesion and a claimable territory. While ethnic heterogeneity made the achievement of class consciousness difficult (perhaps impossible, in the European sense), the absence of controllable physical territory prevented the development of secure local power bases. Labor territory was lacking in two senses. (1) Urban residential patterns and politics were based more on ethnicity than on class. As a result, Irish political machines, for example, were more concerned with taking care of the Irish unemployed than with helping Italian workers keep their jobs, and vice versa. Until the New Deal, many urban political machines were notoriously antiunion. Even socialist city governments, as in Milwaukee, were founded upon a coincidence of ethnic and class interests, in that case German American. (2) The only economic "property" which could be controlled by industrial, as opposed to agricultural labor, was the job itself. Implicit demands for the control of factories, rolling stock and other company property were sometimes expressed (for example, when such property was seized or destroyed), but even during the Michigan sit-down strikes, seizure of auto plants symbolized the demand for control of working conditions and job security rather than for control of the literal means of production. (An analogy is the occupation of university administration buildings by insurgent students.) As domestic Marxists were well aware, occupation of factories without simultaneous control over investment, distribution and marketing facilities was useless, and without at least neutralizing the coercive force of the state, impossible.

There was thus no way in which American workers could achieve quasi-independence without powerful aid. Lacking a defensible territory, they were unable to conduct an independence revolt. Lacking group solidarity, they were equally unable to conduct a revolution. Still, since the causes of violence persisted, so did violence — particularly in those industries in which some degree of group cohesion could be created and some territory defended. Workers in western timber and mining areas engaged in bitter warfare with management from 1892, when the Coeur d'Alene region of Idaho exploded, through the mining wars of Colorado, Nevada and California, the timber battles of the Pacific Northwest and the bitter Appalachian mining fights of the 1920's and 1930's. In isolated mining areas, organization of workers along craft lines was impossible; place of residence and place of work were virtually identical; workers, and their families, despite ethnic differences, could be molded into conscious communities; living and working conditions were unsurpassed in oppressiveness, and local governments, corrupt and brutal, were in the hands of the mineowners. Given the owners' propensity to attack unions by having labor leaders framed, imprisoned or deported, and to break strikes by importing railroad carloads of strikebreakers, and given the presence of militant organizers like Big Bill Haywood of the Western Federation of Miners and John L. Lewis of the United Mine Workers, violence was inevitable. Its intensity may be judged by the fact that federal troops were called out more often in connection with mining disorders than in all other types of labor disturbance combined. Its nature may be illuminated, at least in part, by recalling that the miners sometimes gained *de facto* control of fairly large territorial areas by employing the techniques of organized terrorism. The whole bloody story — from the "bullpens" into which Idaho miners were herded to the Ludlow, Colorado, "tent massacre" of miners' wives and children, and from the assassination of former Idaho governor Frank R. Steunenberg to the trial, acquittal and subsequent deportation of Haywood — cannot be told here. Despite violence and counterviolence, mining and timber workers remained fundamentally powerless until the New Deal.

The Wagner Act — perhaps the most important of all New Deal legislative enactments — placed the entire subject of labor-management relations at once under federal jurisdiction. Unlike other Roosevelt codes which were either invalidated by the Supreme Court or limited in effect to the Depression period, the labor code became a true constitution, as flexible and powerful an instrument of government regulation in 1960 as it had been in 1939. What it represented, however, was not so much a victory for labor as a transformation of labor relations in which both sides gained and lost. By virtue of federal protection, labor won the bare minimum it had so long sought in vain — stable local organization. The large unions' existence was guaranteed by the employers' legal duty to bargain and by legislative procedures designed to force union recognition, after appropriate employee elections, upon both unwilling employers and unwilling employees. Labor also won recognition of the right to strike, to organize free of employer harassment, and to prevent employers from engaging in "unfair labor practices."

In exchange, however, labor gave up more than is generally recognized. The right to strike was counterbalanced by legitimization of management's right to use strikebreakers. The basic "duty to bargain" extended only to matters of wages and working conditions, and gave labor no participation in making basic managerial decisions. Rules concerning "the appropriate bargaining unit" favored decentralization of union power and inter-union competition. Perhaps most important, in tacit exchange for the immediate benefits of organizational security, organized labor acquiesced in a redefinition of the working class. Farm workers, employees in intrastate commerce and other large groups of wage earners were excepted from coverage under the new legislation. Leftists interested in mobilization of the total potential working class were discredited and "purged" from the large national unions. The unions continued their long effort to monopolize existing jobs for their members, trusting the federal government to provide "full employment" after World War II. And, somehow, the beneficiaries of the Roosevelt revolution never did get around to organizing unskilled blacks, or Mexican Americans, or the rural poor.

Nevertheless, with the rise of strategic sectors of the industrial working class to power, the age of intense labor-management violence ended. The next chapter explores the complex relationship between the attainment of power and the termination of political violence. For the present, it is important to recall that, prior to the Depression, organized labor had *not* succeeded in obtaining quasi-independence. Strong local power bases were few, and even where machine bosses and union leaders had learned to tolerate each other (as in New York State) labor was the weaker partner. Even within the Democratic party labor's demands were considered un-American; New York's Al Smith, the Democratic presidential candidate in 1928, was in matters of economics not much to the left of Herbert Hoover, while Franklin D. Roosevelt was initially, in

89

Richard Hofstadter's words, "an acquaintance, not a friend, of organized labor." [6] The breakthrough began around 1936 when, under the pressure of continuing hardship and depression, existing political alignments were shattered and the "second New Deal" began to coalesce around the great unions.

The mid-thirties were immensely turbulent years, with both violence and the threat of violence on the increase. A major race riot shook Harlem in 1935; the rural poor flocked to the banners of Huey Long, Francis E. Townsend and other demagogues; and Communists played an increasingly important role among the urban and industrial poor. With the failure of the National Recovery Administration scheme, big business abandoned Roosevelt entirely; labor, whose left wing was in the process of leaving the AFL to create the CIO, threatened to vote against him in 1936. Despite the overwhelming Democratic victory of that year, labor violence reached new heights in the automobile industry sit-down strikes of 1936 and 1937. Between 1937 and 1940, however, two events occurred which ended the threat of open class warfare: labor's political importance was recognized through implementation of the Wagner Act and related legislation, and the nation began to gear up for war. With the outbreak of World War II the national unity which Roosevelt had sought vainly to enforce through NRA became a reality; and in the virtually uninterrupted twenty-five year boom which followed the war, neither labor nor management found grounds for renewing their old battles on picket lines or in the streets.

What has been described in relatively dispassionate terms was a thoroughgoing social, political, economic and cultural transformation — a period of change so rapid and far-reaching as to break up political party coalitions and make new ones, to alter both the size of government and its relationship to the governed, to create new economic relations among producers and consumers and to change beyond recognition America's role in the world. It is in this process rather than in any specific legislative or political reform that one must seek the answer to the question of how labor-management violence ended. American workers did not rise to power through patience, hard work or the normal operation of "the system" but as a result of unprecedented, often unintended alterations of the system itself. First in the solvent of depression, then in the crucible of war, political and economic institutions were reconstituted on a new basis which, for the first time, admitted elements of organized labor into the ruling coalition. In *The Future of American Politics* Samuel Lubell has described the Roosevelt coalition which emerged from this alchemical caldron; in slightly altered form, regardless of which party is in power, it governs still.[7]

At present, most representatives of the Roosevelt coalition, including organized labor, view their experience during and after the New Deal as prototypal — immediately relevant to problems of conflict resolution in the 1960's. Unfortunately, the outs of the 1930's are the ins of the present era; hence, in describing what happened during and after the New Deal they are tempted to emphasize the mechanical reforms which reflected their achievement of power rather than the process of transformation by which power was actually gained. To take the simplest example, one might say that labor finally triumphed, despite its failure to gain power on the local level, by becoming a specially protected client of the federal government. One might then reason that a similar remedy should solve the problems of black Americans today. But he would be wrong, since blacks are not merely an economic group but a cohesive ethnic group; in their case, favors bestowed by the federal government increase rather than decrease the determination to achieve quasi-independence.

Like organized labor, businessmen dependent upon federal contracts, European immigrant groups, western farmers and other groups which achieved recognition under Roosevelt, modern blacks seek a transformation which will make room for *them* in the ruling coalition. The painful fact which the New Deal's beneficiaries will not recognize openly is that such a transformation would most certainly rock the boat in which they now sail so happily together. Black power in city politics means *less* power for many urban political machines — the same machines which were instrumental in electing Presidents Roosevelt, Truman, Kennedy and Johnson. Black power in the economy means *less* power for many unions, for whom racial discrimination is merely another way of keeping the labor supply short and existing leadership groups in power. Black power in education, welfare, housing construction, the administration of justice and other governmental services means the radical reconstruction of central government bureaucracies which flowered under the New Deal. In short, for blacks, as well as for students, Spanish Americans and other minorities now seeking self-determination, the Roosevelt coalition fulfills the same role played by the forces of status quo prior to 1935 — it offers reform but not reconstruction, change but not transformation. Their dilemma, however, is even more poignant than that of organized labor and the farmers, for if the centralization of power has made quasi-independence impossible, and if the hegemony of the Roosevelt coalition has made the achievement of power at the federal center impossible, what is left save resignation or revolution? This is the question which, in one form or another, will occupy our attention from this point forward.

Responding

Counterforce, Reform

The dilemma faced by modern groups in revolt is not new. Just as money begets money, power begets power; the problem, in either case, is one of primary accumulation. I have suggested that for some groups the achievement of quasi-independence or local autonomy was the road to primary power accumulation, while for others the growth of federal power under the New Deal furnished an escape from powerlessness. Before considering the specific problems and prospects of today's insurgents, it is necessary to deal more generally with the question of how insurgent groups succeed or fail in their struggle for inclusion in the power structure. How have those in power responded to previous domestic revolts? What relationship do such responses bear to the consequences of revolt, for the group and for the larger society? What patterns either of response or of consequence seem relevant to the current period of social conflict and disorder in the United States?

5.

o Group Violence:
nd Transformation

These are difficult questions to ask, let alone answer, since in many cases propositions commonly accepted as "common sense" verities have preempted the field of inquiry. For example, consider the matter of "official violence" or counterforce. One often reads in history books or hears in connection with modern civil disorders the phrase, "The revolt was crushed." The assumption is that revolts are tests of strength, and that the side which kills, incapacitates or intimidates the greatest number of opponents wins. But the evidence is hardly consistent with this assumption. What ends a revolt? The labor movement almost never won a violent battle with management or government troops, yet continued its struggles until after passage of the Wagner Act. Although consistently "crushed," Indian revolts continued until virtually the entire Indian population was killed or herded onto reservations — is this what "crushed" means? The southern defeat in the Civil War did not prevent white southerners from mounting a successful guerrilla campaign two years later, nor has the suppression of riot activity in cities like Watts and Detroit deterred rioters in Chicago and Washington, D.C. Even in the case of individual riots the evidence as to the effectiveness of counterforce is ambiguous. For example, the deployment of city policemen or state troops has often escalated the level of violence (as in New York in 1863, Baltimore in 1877, Chicago in 1894, and 1919, Watts in 1965 and Newark in 1967) while the use of federal troops both in labor and racial riot situations has frequently (but not always) had a de-escalating effect.

It seems, then, that the agency exercising counterforce may have more effect on the individual riot than the level of force employed. Similarly, the method of exercise of counterforce has a significance not generally recognized; given the nature of independence revolts described in Chapter 3, it is not hard to see why sealing off riot areas has generally had more of a "cooling" effect than invading them. In the end, however, it does not appear that any sort of moderate counterforce or counterinsurgency is effective in terminating a *series* of riots which form part of a mass revolt like that of labor or the urban black community. Suppression of one uprising does not deter potential rioters elsewhere. In such circumstances, even sophisticated counterinsurgency seems to backfire, Vietnam style, by compelling insurgent groups to resort to more covert, calculated and decentralized operations. (We will come in a moment to the question of immoderate counterforce.)

In questioning purported "common sense" verities such as the proposition that revolts may be crushed by counterforce, we must also critically scrutinize glib assertions about "official violence" which make it appear that all acts of revolt are, literally, acts of self-defense. Ever since the eighteenth century, those wishing to justify individual instances of revolt on grounds of self-defense have relied on prior acts of violence by those in authority to furnish that justification. In the midst of the Green Mountain Boys' uprising, for example, Ethan Allen wrote the governor of New York: "Though they style us rioters for opposing them, and seek to catch and punish us as such, yet in reality themselves are the rioters, the tumultuous, disorderly, stimulating faction. . . ." [1] Since our interest is in understanding rather than in justifying, we can afford to be more analytical. The problem, first of all, is one of definition, for "official violence" has at least four meanings:

(1) It sometimes means *illegal* acts of violence performed by the representatives of government, for example, acts of police brutality.

(2) In a slightly more metaphorical sense, "official violence" may refer to the illegitimate use of discretion by representatives of government. An example is the discriminatory enforcement of a legal code, as when members of a minority group are arrested and jailed for acts which would not lead to the arrest of members of the majority.

(3) Even more metaphorically, "official violence" sometimes refers to an entire political, legal or economic system which discriminates against and brutalizes an outgroup, for example, a Jim Crow legal system. The "violence" in this case lies in the enforcement of unjust laws, even though that enforcement may involve no more than the usual compulsion exercised by governmental bodies.

(4) Finally, "official violence" may be used to mean the *failure* of the authorities to act so as to protect one group from violent attack by another. Police collusion in white attacks on blacks, which characterized many earlier race riots, may thus be seen as one type of official violence.

Enough has already been said about the causes of domestic political violence to enable one to see that although "official violence" in the literal sense (definition 1) often triggers riots or insurrections, it is systematic coercion (definitions 2, 3 and 4) which constitutes a precondition of group revolt. Oppressive laws oppressively enforced are an integral part of the relationship earlier described as internal colonialism, and it is this relationship rather than specific acts of official violence which generates insurgency. The strategy represented by definition 4, permitting one subject population to keep another in check, is also characteristic of colonial systems; the Romans called it *divide et impera:* divide and rule. But there is much more to a colonial system than oppressive rule, much more than dividing to conquer. There are also the well-intentioned efforts to "develop" the subject population, to "civilize" it and to "integrate" it into a larger peaceful whole. Therefore domestic mass revolt is seldom merely a response to official violence. And, conversely, ending the official violence (in the narrow sense of definition 1) will not necessarily or even probably end the revolt. As Edward W. Gude has suggested, it is *violation* rather than mere violence which provokes mass revolt.[2]

Once a revolt has begun, the most common question is whether "official violence," reform or some combination of counterforce and reform will end it. Military suppression has ended some rebellions, like that of the Indian peoples; capitulation to the insurgents, as in the case of the Reconstruction Klan, terminated others. At most times during their history, however, Americans confronted by violent uprisings have responded more ambiguously, alternating the carrot of moderate reform with the stick of mild suppression. During the ghetto uprisings of the past few years, police and troops called in to suppress disorders have often used excessive violence (as in Newark and Detroit) but have not committed massacres; they have not, for example, turned machine guns on looters. With a few exceptions (like the United States government's treatment of the Indians) this has been the recurrent pattern of suppression: a moderate level of counterforce, marked by violence, but falling short of mass murder or imprisonment of entire groups. And along with relatively mild suppression has gone moderate reform, from the offers of colonial legislatures to remedy some grievances of the Appalachian farmers in the 1770's to the civil rights legislation of the 1960's, enacted in response to southern sit-ins and northern rioting. The problem, however, is that these methods have so seldom been effective in terminating mass revolt. The historical material suggests that once law-abiding Americans reach the point of mass disobedience to law, their revolts will be ended neither by moderate force nor by moderate reform, but may, in fact, be intensified by both.

Both techniques were attempted during the eighteenth-century farmer uprisings, for example, with uprisings in New Jersey, the Carolinas, Pennsylvania, New York and Massachusetts put down in relatively bloodless battles, while legislatures held out the olive branch of compromise. (Captain Daniel Shays, one recalls, was pardoned after leading the Massachusetts rebellion and lived out a long life in self-imposed exile in New York.) Still, until the Jeffersonian accession, farmer uprisings continued to occur. Similarly, the North-West axis which came to control Congress in the decades before the Civil War attempted to end southern insurgency by combining law enforcement (e.g., Jackson's Force Act, passed in response to South Carolinian "nullification") with a series of famous compromises on the issue of slavery. The fate of these compromises is well known, as is the result of the North's attempt to end Reconstruction terrorism without mobilization of all available counterforce. Even during the period of labor-management warfare, the pattern persisted. While the force used to suppress strikes and riots was not massive enough to destroy the labor movement, reforms achieved (recognition of some unions, victory in some strikes and a pro-labor attitude on the part of the Wilson administration) were not sufficient to meet the movement's demands and needs. The revolt therefore continued well into Roosevelt's second administration. Similarly, at present, it appears that gentle enforcement of civil rights laws and court decisions in the South will not integrate southern schools or alter fundamental patterns of racial discrimination in that section, while a similar combination of police action and legislative reform proves ineffective to end the revolt of ghetto blacks in the North.

A clue as to why moderate methods so often fail to terminate domestic revolts is provided by reconsidering the motives of both rebels and authorities. Whether on the frontier or in the factory, in rural southern communities or in urban ghettos, what rebels have demanded is the satisfaction of their *group* interests, including interests in exercising political and economic power and in controlling their own social systems. Metaphorically, as has been noted, these desires translate into "independence" — the integration into American society not just of scattered group members but of the collectivity considered as a cultural, economic, political and, where possible, territorial unit. Prior to and during their struggle for greater autonomy, insurgent groups experience a sharp increase in collective pride and in political awareness. They reject old-style leaders and choose new ones reflecting this fresh awareness. Old links with outside society are seen as obsolete and discarded; new ones are forged in the heat of revolt.

The achievement of a greater degree of local autonomy often facilitates the creation of group economic institutions, speeds up internal modernization, and increases political power based on solidarity (e.g., the "bloc vote").

Paradoxically, therefore, revolts or insurrections seen by those in power as divisive, separatist or even anarchist have often had the effects of restoring social order to the group and reuniting the insurgents on a new basis with the larger body politic. "Independence" implies a new interdependence based no longer on favors asked and received but on the respect which power owes to power. It may be argued, of course, that this is not a final state but a phase of group development. Accepting this notion *arguendo,* it nevertheless seems clear that it is an essential phase; all successful American groups, including WASPs, have passed or are passing through it on their way to maturity and power.

What rebels perceive, and authorities do not, is that in a rapidly changing, modernizing, centralizing society like the United States, a high level of group autonomy is not a dream of glory or a utopia but a prerequisite for survival. Those excluded from power learn quickly that the most desperate competition in America is not between man and man but between group and group, and that those who exercise great power do so on behalf of groups. They know from bitter experience the profound weakness and manipulability of the unaffiliated individual. Therefore the one compromise they will not accept is one which requires them to dissolve collectively and return to a state of unaffiliated individualism.

To those in authority, however, this kind of collectivism seems both anachronistic and dangerous. Those possessing power prefer to think of themselves as individuals, and to credit their success to individual rather than collective achievement. It is convenient for one who has "arrived" to forget that he rose to individual success by standing on the shoulders of a collectivity, and tempting to pretend that power once obtained can be exercised impartially on behalf of the "American people" rather than certain privileged groups. Automatically, it seems, the newly arrived begin to play down their past and present group commitments (or, which is the same thing, to deprive such commitments of political content), to conceive of the "American people" as a relatively undifferentiated mass, to speak of "divisive group nationalism" or "petty localism" and to deny the existence of a power structure composed of cooperating groups. Their solution to the problem of violent mass revolt is to offer the rebels the benefits of individualism — reforms which promise members of the insurgent group fairer treatment, more votes, more jobs, etc. — provided only that they give up "unrealistic" demands for control of territory, recognition of collective political and economic interests, and the like. Naturally, such reforms are usually rejected.

Repeatedly this scenario has been acted out. (1) American colonists, western farmers, southern secessionists, labor union men, urban blacks and others — all were offered the benefit of integration *as individuals* into a pre-existing social system, provided only that they renounce the goal of exercising independent, collective power. (2) In each case compromises embodying individual rather than group integration were rejected as being the equivalent of group death. (3) Rejection of such compromises convinced the authorities in each case that the rebels were both ungrateful and irrational and paved the way for violent confrontation. (4) Attempts to terminate the revolts by suppressing individual uprisings failed, in each case, to end the recurrence of uprisings or to block political development of the insurgent group. (5) What finally terminated each conflict was either massive military suppression or some concatenation of events which so transformed the preexisting social system as to permit integration of the insurgent *group,* and not just some of its members individually, into American society.

It is important to note that, as a rule, the means of such integration have been either accidental or improvised, since an individualistic political and economic system lacked the machinery for advancing the interests of groups *qua* groups. Therefore, methods of group advancement which now seem "traditional" — for example, political parties, urban political machines, business corporations, labor unions, federal agencies and community organizations — were all considered in their inception dangerous and un-American. Moreover, the integration of large out-groups into American society generally took place not as a result of in-group generosity or reform but in the wake of system-transforming "explosions" like westward expansion, civil or world war and depression. What is meant by "transformation" can be illustrated by a few examples.

Farmer violence on the Appalachian frontier ended not because individual uprisings were suppressed, but because between 1799 (the date of the Fries Rebellion) and 1828 (Andrew Jackson's election) a national transformation made room for the exercise of collective power by the West. In fact, just prior to Jefferson's election in 1800 the situation was extremely critical, with workingmen rioting in the cities, Jeffersonian agents at work among insurgent farmers and the Federalists in power resorting to press censorship and political trials (the Alien and Sedition Laws) to stem the tide of change. However, Jefferson's election established the "revolutionary" device of a two-party system (among other radical political reforms) and three years later the Louisiana Purchase gave American farmers a continent to till and rule. The extent of these and other changes in this period of transformation, resulting in a shift of power westward, may be judged by New England's threat (at the Hartford Convention in 1815) to secede from the Union during a war promoted by the new West-South axis.

The *southern independence movement* was broken (and rule by Republican businessmen established) not through moderate reform or mild suppression, but in the bloodiest war ever fought by Americans. Even so, the degree of force employed was not sufficient to deter southerners from rising again during Reconstruction in order to force the North to choose between *de facto* southern independence and massive suppression. In the end, national unity at the federal level was restored by an industrial transformation which put the same interests in control of both political parties, thus enabling southerners to participate in the election of President Grover Cleveland.

Organized labor's rise to power was attributable neither to repeated suppression of labor violence nor to the generosity of employers, but to a depression and a war which transformed America almost beyond recognition. Much the same thing may be said of the small farmers of the West, who in the early 1930's were participating in small uprisings reminiscent of the wars of the Regulators and the Whiskey Rebellion. The same transformation consolidated on a national level the local power gained by immigrant ethnic groups between 1880 and 1930, and made it possible for whole collectivities to rise rapidly into the suburban middle class.

The coincidence of the great age of European immigration (1880–1930) with America's transition from a rural to an urban-industrial society goes far toward explaining why *immigrating ethnic groups* could achieve collective integration into the American economic and political systems without sustained political violence. In effect, these immigrants (particularly the earlier arrivals) came in on the ground floor of industrial expansion and the creation of the modern city. (Even so, the improvisation of urban political machines, often financed by alliances with racketeers, was hardly a nonviolent transformation.) More important, were it not for the further change which made possible a flight to the suburbs after World War II, the cities would probably now be in a state of open civil war. The suburbs were the "second frontier" which functioned after the war much as the Louisiana territory did in Jefferson's day.

Most *American blacks,* however, now live in the cities. The current demand among ghetto residents for black power — greater control by black communities of inner-city school systems, police forces, real estate and commercial opportunities, political organizations and so forth — is a typical example of the drive toward local autonomy which has characterized other American out-groups. (This same drive has motivated, at least in part, several modern domestic revolts, including the student power movement and opposition to racial "integration" by white southerners and urban blue-collar workers.) Typical, too, has been the response of those in authority, who continue to prescribe individualistic remedies for collective grievances. Fair housing in the suburbs, job training, increased educational opportunities, more housing units and bigger welfare checks are remedies no less individualistic for being welfare-state originated.

This situation creates an irony, however, which few in authority perceive or understand. Blacks, students, blue-collar workers and others resort increasingly to violence to express their desperation over a growing lack of control over their communal affairs and their own lives — an increasing dependence on powerful outsiders operating through impersonal bureaucracies. What they require, like groups before them, is a transformation which will make room for the exercise of collective power by *their* members. Such groups are told, however, that the solution to their problem lies in further absorption of individuals into the bureaucracies of big business, big unionism and big government. From the point of view of the technocrats who come increasingly to dominate an advanced industrial society, history is on the side of centralization, modernization and socioeconomic integration. Moves toward local autonomy are romantic delusions, foredoomed to failure by the very nature of technological civilization. The implication, of course, is that since uprisings directed toward greater group autonomy cannot succeed anyway, they ought to be suppressed.

Obviously, the shape of the technological society of the future lies outside the scope of this study. It is worth pointing out, however, that despite several metamorphoses the ideology of the American ruling coalition always points to the same conclusion: dissolution of the out-group demanding recognition. The argument from history is nothing new; it was used by northerners against southerners, by industrialists against labor unionists (in the form of social Darwinism), by Republicans against Populists and by Progressives against immigrants demanding control of city political machines. The interests in power have a large stake in convincing out-groups that history, or the gods, has put everyone in his proper place, and that to demand system transformation is to swim against the stream of history or fate. Nevertheless, our historical evidence shows that rebellious out-groups continue to battle for their collective survival against all odds, and not always unsuccessfully. If moderate reform will not alter their goals nor sap their will, neither, it is certain, will arguments from history.

Failing system transformation sufficient to permit an outgroup to wield collective power, the question is whether official violence will terminate a violent revolt. It seems clear, as stated previously, that *moderate* force — the usual response of authority groups to domestic violence — is no more effective in accomplishing this aim than moderate reform. In fact, as example after example shows, the initial failure of moderate force to do the job often results in escalation by the authorities, counterescalation by the rebels, and a cycle of violence which ends either in official withdrawal or virtual destruction of the insurgent group. The process by which spontaneous mass rioting becomes progressively more destructive as official violence escalates is a familiar one. Moreover, if official violence escalates to the point of attempting to break up the insurgent group (as by infiltrating its organizations or arresting its leadership), a turn toward more calculated, highly organized terrorism can be predicted. In most instances of group revolt described thus far, insurgents have moved from civil disobedience through spontaneous mass rioting to organized terrorism.

The reasons for the failure of moderate or even escalated force to end such revolts become clearer when one recognizes that these episodes of mass violence are not expressions of aimless criminality but of essentially political demands. Indeed, political violence is a form of speech beyond speech; it is the language of the mute and powerless. The force employed in order to deter individuals from engaging in criminal activities — for example, the threat of arrest and imprisonment — will not deter insurgents from engaging in political violence. Such violence is based on a collective perception that "law and order" is not neutral and sacred but a servant of the interests which wield it. Therefore, violent uprisings often contain within the forms of anarchy a seed of order: the implicit appeal to a "higher law" of self-determination and compensation for past injustice suffered. In the later stages of revolt arrests and sentences may become badges of honor. Small wonder that ordinary criminal procedures rarely deter the rebels from continuing to fight.

But if ordinary deterrent procedures are unavailing, what will stop the revolt? Typically, the authorities come to rely more and more on punitive rather than deterrent techniques — for example, beating rioters or demonstrators rather than arresting them, jailing insurgent leaders for long periods of time (or, where possible, deporting them), and retaliating against the insurgent community-at-large where individual suspects cannot be found. Throughout this period of struggle the authorities are limited and hampered by attempts to stretch normal criminal law and constitutional procedures to cover the exigencies of suppressing a political revolt. As we have seen, so long as the basic conditions of the insurgency remain unaltered, these efforts generally accomplish little but the conversion of mass rioting into organized terrorism, as rebel leaders are driven underground and the community further alienated from the law. The next step, short of official withdrawal or a system transformation, may be massive suppression of the insurgency — the dissolution of the group by force. At this point, the authorities cease to speak of "police action" and begin to think and act in terms of "war."

There is little use trying to pretend in the name of liberalism or humanitarianism that official violence never accomplishes anything. On the contrary, our history shows that domestic political revolts may be permanently suppressed by force, *provided that society is willing to pay the price* — escalation of official violence to official terror and destruction of the rebellious group as a political entity. Almost all of the excesses of official violence which Americans like to attribute to German fascism, for example, have been practiced at one time or another against domestic groups.

With the approval of the government in Washington, southern whites effectively militarized their entire society between 1830 and 1860, terminating the education of Negro slaves and depriving them of human rights, restricting their movements and punishing real or alleged revolts by summary execution of suspects. Mob violence tacitly sanctioned by the government was employed with terrible effect against the West Coast Chinese and Japanese as well as against southern blacks in the decades following the Civil War. Systematic political persecution by government — using the techniques of discriminatory legislation, nighttime raids, mass deportation, officially condoned mass violence and jailing of political prisoners — was employed against rebellious political minorities like the IWW socialists of 1917–1922. During the First World War, all Germans were suspected of disloyalty and many were physically attacked or had property destroyed by mobs; during the Second World War, virtually the entire West Coast Japanese community was removed by the United States government to detention camps in the West. Most violent of all, however, was the two-hundred-and-fifty-year campaign of suppression waged against the American Indians, the one example in our history of official violence raised to a genocidal scale within the United States. This struggle deserves particular attention in the light of contemporary events, for it provides us with a set of conditions for massive military suppression of a large racial minority.

A fundamental precondition for such suppression is intense animosity, economic competition and violent conflict between an excluded, rebellious out-group and a *former* out-group on its way to power. For almost two centuries the principal source of pressure on the Indians was not the United States government but land-hungry white settlers; however, the farmers' rise to power between 1760 and 1830 forced officialdom to recognize their interests and to abandon the cause of the Indian. As early as the 1670's, Virginia settlers, led by Nathaniel Bacon, had engaged in an armed insurrection against their governor, largely because of his pro-Indian policies and failure to preserve law and order on the frontier. The first act of the United States Army after independence was to put down an Indian revolt in the Ohio Valley, and when the farmers came to power, the United States government came actively into the struggle, crushing a series of rebellions and then "removing" the Indians to territory west of the Mississippi (whence they would be removed again to reservations, and decimated when they rebelled). Thus, ironically, was the displacement and slaughter of the Indians linked with the rise of mass democracy, as pressure from below forced official violence to become both more official and more violent. Much the same thing was true of the influence of poor whites on southern governments with regard to suppression of Negroes; and contemporary pressure now being exerted on both political parties by lower-middle-class whites (based in part on competition for land and jobs) is analogous.

Massive suppression of a large domestic group is psychologically impossible, however, without extreme racism. The members of the out-group to be destroyed must first be considered collectively inferior, then un-American or "alien," and then subhuman. As soon as the assumption is made that the group is essentially alien, a revolt may be interpreted not as a method of gaining collective admission to the society but as an attack on the United States. Military action against the group then becomes "self-defense" and the conflict "war." Thus it is not customary even to consider Indian revolts under the heading "domestic violence," so accustomed are we to assuming the red man's *a priori* foreignness. There was, of course, a legal basis for considering Indians both foreigners and subwhite; "treaties" had been negotiated within the Indian "nations" ever since colonial days, and the Constitution provided that an Indian, like a Negro, should be counted as three-fifths of a white man for purposes of apportionment of representatives and taxes. But the legal trappings reflected a tacit agreement among whites to *continue* to exclude Indians from the body politic no matter how "white" or domesticated they became. Among the first victims of official removal were the Creeks and Cherokees, peaceful farming people so "white" in attitude that, in some cases, they owned Negro slaves!

This agreement, in turn, appears to have been based on several widely shared assumptions: that Indians were incapable of being Europeanized, that the American way of life and the Indian way of life were incompatible and that it was a case of "kill or be killed." In part, these assumptions reflected absurd stereotypes, such as the idea that all Indians were nomadic hunters, or that they were incapable of rational thought. In part, however, they were true: many Indians did not want to ape the white man; many did not want to eliminate their tribal and multitribal organization to become individuated Christians and capitalists. All this helped to prove even to the best-intentioned soul-savers that the ungrateful natives must be relocated or destroyed (or both). Most whites never considered making

111

radical changes in their society to accommodate the Indians' basic needs or demands. Only a few missionaries had the slightest glimmerings that it might be possible, for example, to control the cheating of Indians by white speculators, or to permit communal ownership of land to continue within the framework of capitalism, or to treat the great Indian tribes not as foreign "nations" but as quasi-independent political groups similar to corporations.

Whatever small chances the eighteenth-century visionaries might have had to convince others that these were not vain dreams were destroyed by the Indian revolts beginning in 1793, which reconfirmed the already widespread belief in Indian baseness and unassimilability. The classic racist cycle was completed: a people excluded by white Americans as alien attempt to defend what is left of their territory and their group existence by rebelling. Whites, now adopting the defense of necessity, interpret the revolts as proof that the rebels are hostile aliens who must be destroyed.

This analysis may help us to understand why many modern blacks worry about genocide, for although neither precondition for massive suppression of blacks by whites yet exists, both could materialize in a comparatively short time. Southerners, members of competing ethnic groups, ideological racists and others who might generate pressure for such suppression failed to make significant inroads into the electorate in the presidential campaign of 1968. Although they did compel both major party candidates to pay verbal homage to "law and order," they do not yet control the government. Moreover, although racism in the sense of hostility toward blacks is rife, most whites remain committed to the idea that black people are excluded Americans rather than unassimilable aliens. Nevertheless, the situation remains fraught with danger. As moderate reform fails to create the kind of fundamental change which would permit a greater degree of group autonomy among blacks, militant nationalists call for a separate state and revolutionaries preach guerrilla warfare. As moderate force fails to end the turmoil, whites become impatient and "law and order" candidates are elected to office. The inadequacy of moderate measures to terminate wars of group liberation confronts those in authority with a choice between radical political change and radical suppression; and there is clearly a strong temptation to adopt the latter course. Already police force political groups begin to remind one of Nat Bacon's army, while voices reminiscent of Indian-fighting days suggest that if blacks want community control they can have it — on policed urban "reservations."

Even more ominously, moderate, middle of the road observers, baffled by the ineffectiveness of halfway measures of both reform and law enforcement, have begun to think in terms of escalation of both. As in Vietnam, there is a tendency to escalate military action against the rebels while attempting simultaneously to speed up the pace of reform — but, again as in Vietnam, it proves impossible both to save and destroy the same peasants. The road to massive suppression is paved with strategic hamlets and reservations, more livable ghettos and cleaner jails, counter insurgency forces and riot control squads. Witnessing the arming of police departments with sophisticated weaponry, the increase in paramilitary activity among white citizens, the infiltration of political groups by security police, the attempts to disarm street gangs and the arrest or assassination of militant black leaders, many blacks have begun to see both increased suppression and ineffective reformism as part of a single genocidal plan. Thus, the atmosphere of "kill or be killed" builds on both sides, along with pressure for a "first strike." It is extremely disturbing to learn, as Dr. John Spiegel of Brandeis University has reported, that the incidence of racial violence with political overtones increased in 1968 over 1967, notwithstanding that there were fewer major riots in 1968 than in 1967. The implication is that violence is becoming more decentralized and quotidian — a predictable turn of events in the absence of meaningful change in the conditions of ghetto life.

Armageddon, of course, is not yet with us. In the black community it may still be avoided. But America's problem, as I have tried to suggest, is not so much black violence, student violence or official violence as it is *group* violence created by the systematic colonization of outgroups. Blacks, students and every other excluded group presently in revolt may succeed in gaining full admission to the American political, economic and social communities without altering by one iota the nature of internal colonialism. In fact, this is one of the most familiar patterns in our history: the colonized of yesterday become the colonizers of tomorrow, politely interested in the welfare of new outgroups, worried about law and order, but unwilling to jeopardize their own hard-won status by risking a political transformation. No doubt the beneficiaries of the next transformation will be shocked by the emergence of mass violence on the part of small farmers, perhaps, or the rural poor, or women seeking recognition as a political force. No doubt they will study the "small farmer problem" or the "women's rights problem" just as we study the black problem and the student problem. Little gain will have been made, however, unless we have in the meantime begun to solve the *colonial* problem by building into American society and American politics the means for assuring peaceful power transference to emerging groups.

"I we could first know where we are, and whither we are tending, we could better judge what to do and how to do it." Thus spoke Abraham Lincoln in the heat of a sensational contest two years before the outbreak of civil war. By contrast, most modern government officials and administrators, forced to respond quickly both to violence and to political pressure, have little time for self-questioning. Action is an unceasing is out. The results are unfortunate: courses of action whose advisability seems self-evident are frequently made, notwithstanding that in our present state of ignorance nothing about political violence is self-evident. Most of all its issues. Even where official analyses are undertaken, analysts tend to adopt a violence-management perspective, defining the problems of political violence in such a way as to make them amenable to solution by quick government action. This book, I hasten to add, does not contain "the answer" either, but it does per-

"*I*f we could first know where we are, and whither we are tending, we could better judge what to do and how to do it." Thus spoke Abraham Lincoln in the heat of a senatorial contest two years before the outbreak of civil war. By contrast, most modern government officials and administrators, forced to respond quickly both to violence and to political pressure, have little time for self-questioning. Acting is in; theorizing is out. The results are unfortunate: countermoves whose advisability seems self-evident are frequently made, notwithstanding that in our present state of ignorance nothing about political violence is self-evident, least of all its "cure." Even where official analyses are undertaken, analysts tend to adopt a violence-management perspective, defining the problems of political violence in such a way as to make them amenable to solution by quick government action. This book, I hasten to add, does not contain "the answer" either, but it does per-

6.

The Ghetto Revolt:
A Crisis of Colonialism

mit us to approach the ghetto revolt from a somewhat different perspective.

The reader will recall that in the early history of urban race riots racial disorder (meaning attacks by whites against blacks) was often a highly charged form of labor violence. From the Cincinnati riot of 1828 (in which half the Negro population was driven out of town) until the bloody East St. Louis affray of 1917 (generated by use of Negro strikebreakers to defeat striking aluminum workers), white working people, both "native" and "immigrant," struck out against those who threatened to reduce their status and pay through wage competition. Their attacks against Negroes followed closely the pattern of black immigration; during the Civil War and immediately afterward, black communities in border state cities like Memphis, Cincinnati and Louisville, as well as in New York, were prey to white mobs supported by law enforcement

117

officials who "looked the other way." These riots were more like massacres than like later communal disorders, since the blacks could not, or would not retaliate. The National Advisory Commission on Civil Disorders, in relating the history of the East St. Louis riot, described a scene typical of this first phase of urban racial violence:

. . . *streetcars were stopped, and Negroes, without regard to age or sex, were pulled off and stoned, clubbed and kicked, and mob leaders calmly shot and killed Negroes who were lying in blood in the street. As the victims were placed in an ambulance, the crowds cheered and applauded.*[1]

White attacks on Negro neighborhoods continued with the great wave of race riots of 1919, but now the pattern altered significantly. Whites were incited to violence not just by black competition for jobs but by the entire set of complaints described earlier as "nativist": increasing job competition, expansion of black residential areas, increased crime and gang warfare, alleged declines in moral standards and property values, and a nascent threat to the white political power structure. And now the Negroes retaliated when attacked. In the Chicago riot, the most destructive of this series (others took place in Omaha, Knoxville, Charleston, Washington, D.C. and Longview, Texas), fifteen whites and twenty-three blacks were killed in waves of white attack and black counterattack. During one turbulent week, whites assaulted Negroes going to and from their jobs, or drove through the ghetto shooting bystanders, while, for their part, the blacks attacked whites found in or near their territory, including policemen. Six thousand troops brought in by Mayor William Thompson as the rioting waned were successful in protecting the ghetto from further invasion. However, further riots involving white attack and Negro retaliation took place in subsequent years, culminating in the Detroit riot of 1943 which took a toll of twenty-five Negro and white deaths, with destruction of property valued at well over two million dollars. Communal riots of this type still occur, but beginning with the Harlem riot of 1943 (so vividly described in Ralph Ellison's novel *Invisible Man*) racial disorder entered its third phase.

During each summer from 1964 through 1968, violence erupted in major American cities. Although the Kerner Commission has identified several hundred disorders in as many cities during this period, the major outbreaks took place in Rochester, New York and Philadelphia (1964), Los Angeles (1965), Chicago and Cleveland (1966), Newark, northern New Jersey cities and Detroit (1967). In the spring of 1968, while this book was in preparation, similar uprisings in Baltimore, Washington, D.C., Pittsburgh, Chicago and more than twenty other locations were triggered by the assassination of Dr. Martin Luther King, Jr.

In reporting on the 1967 outbreaks the National Advisory Commission on Civil Disorders (Kerner Commission) stated correctly that there was no "typical riot" or "typical rioter" in the literal sense. There were important variations from city to city depending upon the time and location of the outbreaks, the strategy of law-enforcement forces, and other factors. One can distinguish, for example, between two- and three-day riots (Bedford-Stuyvesant, Cleveland, Washington, D.C. or Chicago, for example) and week-long riots (Watts, Newark, Detroit) on the ground that, in the latter, police or National Guard responses amounted to punitive counterattacks which helped spread both arson and sniping into residential areas. Nevertheless, what strikes the historian or social scientist studying the various outbreaks is not their diversity but their similarity. Counterforce strategies or the immediate motivation of rioters might make a great deal of difference in terms of how many lives were lost or the extent of property damage done, but the basic patterns of rioting and response, qualitatively speaking, were in most cases strikingly similar.

In the first place, the major disturbances seemed to proceed through similar stages of mutual escalation: (1) Some act of real or alleged police brutality or other insult to ghetto residents draws a crowd, which begins to harrass the police. (2) Police reinforcements arrive and arrests are made; policemen are stoned and looting of white-owned stores begins. (3) Looting continues, stores are burned and state troopers or National Guardsmen (sometimes both) are brought into the area. (4) The arson spreads to whole blocks of stores, residential buildings and housing projects; there is sporadic sniping at troops and firemen. (5) Deployment of federal troops follows to seal off the riot area, after which the violence declines (or "burns out") rapidly.

In addition, the rioting was everywhere spontaneous (that is, not incited by agitators or planned in advance), directed at the same targets (policemen, firemen, white-owned stores and apartment houses), and limited to inner-city ghetto areas. Nowhere were public transportation, heavy industry or defense installations attacked, nor were there attempts by blacks to break out into suburban areas. The response of the authorities was in every case to escalate gradually without sanctioning the massacre of rioters, and to offer negotiations or reforms without promising radical change. Black violence was too localized to be "revolutionary," white suppression too ambivalent and measured to be "counterrevolutionary." This strange and yet familiar embrace suggests that patterns previously discussed as characteristic of domestic political violence are indeed relevant to understanding the Negro revolt. It seems clear that the ghetto revolt was a classical type of response to internal colonialism.

Consider first the size and significance of the great South-to-North black migration of 1940–1960. In two decades more than three million Negroes, most with the skills and customs of a rural peasantry, made the trek into the "promised land" of already overcrowded northern ghettos. This migration ranks in size with the greatest waves of European immigration into American cities. Although World War I had also been followed by a sizable emigration from South to North, the modern history of urban blacks as a colonized people begins with the monumental population shift of 1940–1960. For it was this immigration wave, combined with the political and economic conditions prevailing after World War II, which brought blacks and whites into close contact in the cities, and into a relationship which can accurately be described as internal-colonial. The extent to which intelligent observers tend to underrate the importance of aggressive colonialism in producing the Negro revolt is illustrated by these remarks of a contemporary historian:

. . . it is still not clear whether the ghettos in their present state of inferiority and dependence are in some sense necessary for the functioning of American society — that is, whether powerful interests have a stake in perpetuating them — or whether they persist because American society can get along so well without black people that there is no motive either to integrate them by getting rid of the ghettos or to allow the ghettos to govern themselves. In other

words, what interests have a stake in maintaining the present state of affairs? [2]

We may arrive at some sort of answer to this question by asking another: In what way did the relationship between black ghettos and white groups in power alter between 1945 and 1965? What white "interests" came into play in the ghetto during and after the great migration which had not been significant theretofore? The list is very long, but these examples will suffice.

First, and most obviously, ghetto land, which had not been considered valuable before 1945, rose in value dramatically in the 1950's. With a geometrically increasing Negro population in desperate need of housing, rental and purchase prices of slum buildings soared; in addition, a public housing industry was created. Affluent whites interested in moving back into the city from the suburbs increased the demand for living space, pushing the less affluent into the lower-rent districts on the ghetto fringe. The consequent rise in land values did not go unnoticed by white real estate interests — suppliers, builders, bankers, construction workers, speculators, brokers, landlords — who together form a much larger and more powerful interest group than is generally realized. Allied with government officials and agencies, they moved into the ghettos, demanding and receiving favorable tax treatment, effective immunity from local laws governing building maintenance and rent control, and the power to determine the content of urban renewal programs. Indeed, urban renewal itself became a grab bag, and the Federal Housing Administration an open ally of the real estate interests. Slum clearance was popularly known as "nigger removal" and public housing took a backseat to private development. While a housing boom added 16.8 million new units nationally between 1950 and 1960, the inner cities gained only 2.5 million units, many of which were high or middle-income dwellings.

In the cities, the housing interests fought to maintain outmoded laws favorable to landlords, and decried proposals for reform (whether the object was to facilitate Negro home ownership or to permit government take-overs of slum dwellings) as "socialistic." A favorite tactic of some white landowners was to sell desperately needed housing to blacks on contract for two or three times the appraised value of the property — a bargain which blacks were compelled to accept because of the refusal of both the FHA and mortgage banks to lend them money. In the suburbs, when not practicing "blockbusting" to drive land prices down so that they could be driven up again for blacks, the housing interests were in the forefront of the struggle against open occupancy. By 1968, real estate and its allies were so firmly entrenched in local and federal bureaucracies, both Democratic and Republican, that no one save a handful of black power theorists dared attack them openly — not even the Kerner Commission, whose proposals for housing reform seemed limited to those which would not unduly threaten the developers.

Second, the enormous increase in ghetto population created a vast new market for goods and services, and most of all, given the low or irregular income of most ghetto residents, for credit. Although inner-city residents did not share equitably in postwar prosperity, like everyone else they hungered for goods, both the "necessities" of modern life — the automobile, frozen food, the television set, the telephone, the refrigerator — and the necessities of life in a permanent slum — liquor, drugs, stylish clothes and firearms. The cost of doing business in the ghetto was high, but a large number of entrepreneurs (both white and black) realized that prices and interest rates could be held correspondingly high, particularly with the cooperation or mere inaction of sympathetic government agencies. Whether or not ghetto merchants were "exploiting" blacks in the sense that their profit margins were greater than merchants doing business outside the ghetto (a subject of intense debate) is irrelevant for our purposes. In either case, the result of ghetto capitalism was to hook the poor on goods as so many were hooked on drugs, to deepen poverty and dependence and to discourage the search for more humane methods of producing and consuming goods in poor areas.

The economic pattern is well known. Businessmen whose families had long since moved out of the inner city held on to valuable retail businesses rather than selling out to newer residents. Loan companies took advantage of vague or unenforced usury laws to charge high interest rates both to individuals and ghetto businesses. Sellers of automobiles, furniture, household appliances and other durable goods found it profitable to ask for no money down, charge high interest rates and repossess the property (with the aid of laws favorable to sellers of goods) at the first default in payment. Supermarkets found that they could get rid of inferior or even spoiled merchandise at high prices in ghetto areas; gangsters operated illegal enterprises with the connivance of bribed police and government officials. Like the real estate interests, inner-city entrepreneurs, merchants and credit agencies found friends in high places who helped to preserve the profitable status quo.

Third, the new residents of the ghetto entered cities generally dominated by Democratic political organizations whose principal interest, as far as Negroes were concerned, was to provide just enough direct benefits to keep ghetto

votes in line. Negro politicians acceptable to city machines
were those who would not be too vociferous in demanding
economic or social justice for their people, and who could
keep their constituents satisfied by "delivering the goods"
when pressed to do so. A greatly expanded army of governmental functionaries dealt with ghetto problems in a
similar manner — they acted so as to alleviate suffering
among the poor, but never at the price of their jobs.
Welfare workers, for example, operated under highly complex and often unjust regulations whose simplification —
or outright elimination — their unions opposed. City public school officials and teachers' unions bitterly resisted demands for changes in the school system structure and cur-
riculum, closing the New York City schools for several
months in order to defeat a proposed decentralization plan
there. Police officials, whose small forces had for years
avoided ghetto areas, now found themselves leading miniature armies into battle against black crime; combining a
military mentality with developing political organization,
they also fought to insulate themselves against community
control. Ward heelers and building inspectors, fire chiefs
and liquor licensors — all manner of public servants
fastened themselves securely to the black body politic. Intended to help the patient survive, they fattened themselves
in the bargain.

The contrast between white attitudes towards urban
black communities before and after the Second World War
is well illustrated by variations in police behavior in the
two periods. As almost any police department veteran will
testify, practice in the prewar years was to avoid the ghetto
whenever possible. "If those niggers wanted to cut each
other up on Friday nights," one former policeman told me,
"we weren't about to stop them." By contrast, the postwar
period saw an extraordinary burst of energy and enthusi-

asm directed toward restoring "law and order" in the ghetto, with the result that the police presence in most large black communities now reminds one strongly of an armed occupation. Presumably, the police are no more interested than of old in preventing blacks from cutting each other up; but there is now a bourgeoisie in the ghetto, not to mention a class of absentee owners, which requires protection. Moreover, as has been noted, it is characteristic of colonizers to confer on the colonized both the benefits and burdens of their law, in order to integrate them individually, and over a long period of time, into the existing social system. (The French response to demands for Algerian independence was "Algérie Française" — the integration of Algeria into France.) Expanding legal opportunities for the colonized while stepping up an invasion of their territory is one of the most familiar tactics of colonialists, foreign or domestic.

Official reports on the ghetto riots have emphasized the importance of the 1940–1960 migration, but their failure to perceive and describe the white thrust into the ghetto (as opposed to simple prejudice and exclusionary tactics) has vitiated many of their conclusions. For example, this failure made it possible for the members of the Kerner Commission to view the riots as a form of protest against exclusion and the "two societies" rather than as a revolt aimed at replacing white rule with some form of self-determination. Surely, however, blacks in revolt between 1964 and 1969 were obeying the anticolonial impulse familiar to students of the American Revolution and farmer uprisings, the Civil War and labor-management violence: they fought to rid their territory of the alien, to destroy his works and to reclaim what they felt was rightly theirs. The sentiment was summed up by Bob Bailey of CORE, observing the Watts uprising:

When I saw the police, and they were standing off — way off and wouldn't come down — I felt free for the first time in my life. I felt like I was really part of America, and America was part of me. And that if this is what the white people have been feeling all these years, what a wonderful thing it must be!

I'd participated in the civil rights movement, but I'd never felt that way before. And it seemed to me that this was what America was all about. I felt like I had the Constitution in my brain and that my body and soul were part of the land — that I owned it and wanted to plant flowers and make it green and beautiful. And I ran in the park with the kids and shouted Hallelujah! Hallelujah! [3]

All the preconditions for anticolonial revolt were present in the ghettos of the early 1960's. Urban blacks, a formerly isolated and despised out-group, were brought into close contact with more aggressive, powerful and modern social classes. Under the twin pressures of displacement and colonization, traditional social and religious institutions with roots in the rural South withered; the young *sabras* of the ghetto (who were the principal rioters) were isolated both from traditional past and modern present. The same white invasion which raised group expectation by offering a vision of middle-class life in an integrated America deepened the dependence of blacks upon the white community, for whether the colonizer was a venal slumlord or a do-good welfare worker, the result — increasing dependence — was the same.

Moreover, despite their increasing political awareness, urban blacks were actually falling farther and farther behind their white counterparts. Compared with the average white man, the inner-city Negro was earning less money, going to school for a shorter time and working fewer hours in 1965 than in 1950! Still relative to whites, the black birth rate was increasing radically over these years, and so was the rate of serious crime, infant mortality, disease in general and suicide. In fact, the new generation of ghetto *sabras* was experiencing something new in America — a decline in living standards from one generation to the next. The traditional success story of the American immigrant group was being reversed; and in this context, the occasional successes — or leaps into the middle class — of black businessmen, entertainers, athletes and educators seemed worse than irrelevant. As the 1960's wore on, educational facilities in the ghetto continued to deteriorate. Unemployment continued at major depression levels. Labor unions continued to exclude blacks from apprenticeship programs. The supply of decent housing grew steadily shorter.

As stated earlier, the internal colonial relationship has always been characterized by the enforced dependence of the mass of the colonized upon their masters, while a trickle of talented "natives" are permitted to escape in order to join the middle class. Social psychologists confirm that many ghetto residents have felt for years like children — helpless, fearful, dependent on the white "parents'" favors for their very survival.[4] Young men in particular have been degraded by this lack of control over their own lives — by their inability to get or keep jobs and the need to send their women out to "clean Goldberg's floor," by the "man in the house" policy of the welfare system, by dependence on alcohol and other self-destructive pleasures, and by participation in white exploitation of their black brothers. The guilt produced by complicity in this system provides a strong motivation for revolt, for in rioting and the politics of defiance many find a symbolic liberation from the helplessness, inferiority and guilt produced by dependence. Even looting has psychological value. The window is broken and the old taboos violated; for a moment, at least, the looter is relieved of his burden of dependence on "the Man." This does not mean, however, that rioters have any strong desire to repeat the experience. In fact, the riot seems to lead most rebels, including black rebels, away from mass violence and toward more conventional politics.

All of this information, and more, is contained in reports on urban conditions like those of the National Crime Commission, the Kerner Commission and the National Advisory Commission on the Causes and Prevention of Violence. It has not been used, however, to demonstrate the essentially self-defensive, reactive and anticolonial nature of ghetto revolt (or the links between ghetto revolt and prior American revolts) precisely because such a conclusion would lead by necessary implication to recommendations not capable of easy implementation by the present ruling coalition. If the black revolt is anticolonial, for example, it will be necessary to admit that reforms like more jobs, education and housing will *not* end it (and may even inflame it further) so long as the forces which deepen black dependence remain unchecked. Later, we shall try to describe more clearly what this means in policy terms. For now, however, it is worth pointing out how post-riot developments generally not described in official reports bear out the anticolonialist thesis of urban violence.

Four aftereffects of riots have been particularly noticeable in most large ghettos: increased political awareness on a mass basis, formation of new political, economic and cultural organizations, intensified internal conflict, and greater black solidarity vis-à-vis the outside world. They are closely interrelated, and illustrate my earlier statement that the riots lead toward, not away from political order.

Ghetto uprisings tend to undermine the established Negro leadership, or to provide evidence that that leadership no longer represents many of the black poor. Blacks increasingly interested in ways of expressing their new group consciousness cast about for new leaders, who compete vigorously (and sometimes violently) for their loyalty. As a result, political awareness is further stimulated. In the confusion, it is difficult to tell who really "represents" the black community. This cannot be settled until constituencies have been defined and internal conflicts further resolved. Additionally, in the post-riot period, old links with white society, whether individual or institutional, rapidly become obsolete. New links are created, often in the form of black coalitions presenting a united front to the outsider. Violence, in a sense, is institutionalized; it becomes part of the internal struggle for control of the streets and the masses, and part of the political rhetoric directed towards outsiders. It may become even further institutionalized (as we shall see in a moment) in the form of guerrilla warfare.

In 1968–1969 these post-riot developments were in evidence throughout the nation. Everywhere black leaders reported increased political interest and organization — a proliferation of groups running from businessmen's alliances and black labor unions to new street organizations. Studies of black "militancy" by social scientists showed political awareness, cultural nationalism, willingness to organize and willingness to take to the streets all on the rise, particularly among the young.[5] (In several cities black high school students led strikes, boycotts and street action to protest conditions in the schools.) Intensified conflict both between leaders and between politically ambitious groups was obvious; in Los Angeles, for example, a bitter street war raged between followers of Ron Karenga's US organization and members of the Black Panther party. Nevertheless, like Washington, D.C., Detroit, New York and other cities, Los Angeles witnessed at the same time the formation of a black coalition or "united front" representing all shades of opinion left of the old civil rights organizations and right of the revolutionaries. Moreover, with the outbreak of violent confrontations between black students and white-dominated administrations at Northwestern University, San Francisco State College, Brandeis University, Cornell and elsewhere, the gap between black leaders within the ghetto and student leaders outside it also began to close, while organized Negro policemen in half a dozen major cities declared their intention to be "black first and policemen second." Paradoxically, therefore, the same process which produced intensified infighting generated a heightened sense of unity in the face of the common enemy.

The authorities invariably assume that civil disorder will produce accelerating social disorganization, disrespect for law and, ultimately, anarchy, whereas, again and again in American history, the violence associated with decolonization has led in the direction of a new politics and a reconstructed social order. Recalling American political life in the 1790's, politics on the frontier in the 1820's and 1830's, Reconstruction government in the South and the activities of political machines after their take-over by immigrant groups, one might say that the direction of such movements has been from political violence to a violent type of politics. Blacks, like earlier insurgents, clearly do *not* seek to replace order with disorder or law with anarchy; the one riot report which favored this view (the McCone Commission report on the Watts riot) has by now been discredited both methodologically and politically. The colonial world, Fanon said, "is a world cut in two," but blacks do not seek merely to end the "two societies" through individual integration into white society, any more than Algeria sought to end her servitude to France through integration as a *département* of the Republic. It is group liberation which is sought, the recognition of the black subnation in a society of subnations, the achievement of group rather than individual equality. This is why post-riot developments show not only an awakening to the realities of the colonial situation but a collective effort to reconstruct the relationship between black and white communities on a noncolonial basis.

The emergence of sporadic terrorist activity in at least five cities during the summer of 1968 (Cleveland, Chicago, Philadelphia, Los Angeles and San Francisco) might appear to contradict what has been said previously about the increasing politicization of the black community. It does not, in fact, since in the period of decolonization (which is far from ended) revolutionaries are one of the emerging leadership groups competing for mass loyalty. Terrorism, in other words, is another form of violent politics.

Earlier, the reader will recall, we found that certain groups moved fairly rapidly from violence of the unplanned, spontaneous type to selective terrorism — the planned commission of acts of violence and intimidation by small armed cadres supported passively by a substantial number of the subject population. This happened (in the case of the Ku Klux Klan, for example) where the political consciousness of the insurgents was already high and authority clearly unresponsive to their demands. The critical question for the analyst is whether black guerrillas will be supported by a number of the ghetto population sufficiently large to permit the establishment of and to provide sanctuary for effective terrorist organizations. We have learned in Vietnam that where a subject population feels sufficiently alienated from those in authority, revolutionaries combining persuasion and intimidation may come to be viewed by a large segment of the people as their "legitimate" representatives. When this occurs, saboteurs become heroes and sheltering them becomes an act of patriotism; "selling out" or collaboration in any form is a sin against one's people; and no end to the struggle will suffice save victory or death. We also know, thanks to Vietnam, that where this process is far enough advanced, an antirevolutionary government must be prepared virtually to exterminate the rebels in order to maintain power, since counterinsurgency short of genocide will only strengthen the solidarity of the oppressed.

To say that some terrorism has already occurred, however, is not to say that the stage of mass support for armed cadres has been reached. That it has *not* yet been reached is proved by the continued sale of information by ghetto residents to the police, the refusal of most street organizations to be converted to revolutionary ideals, and the fact that would-be guerrillas do not yet feel ready to launch sustained attacks against policemen, industrial plants, public property or whites outside the ghetto. What does seem to be occurring now is a desperate fight within the black community which, together with white responses, will ultimately determine which kind of leadership the ghetto masses are to follow.

As Charles V. Hamilton has stated, revolutionaries are but one of the Negro elites now seeking to create (perhaps "discover" would be a better word) mass constituencies. "Political bargainers" like Mayor Hatcher of Gary, Indiana, advocate advancing the Negro cause through nonvio-

lent electoral techniques. "Moral crusaders" like Coretta
King and Dr. Ralph Abernathy of SCLC preach peaceful
civil disobedience and legislative reform. "Radical reformers" (Roy Innis of CORE or Eldridge Cleaver of the Black
Panther party) want drastic political, economic and social
change in the direction of community self-determination
and active revolutionaries (anonymous) practice terrorism.[6] Despite the present infighting and general confusion
characterizing ghetto politics, the major struggle now developing pits the first three potential leadership groups
against the last, for while radical reformers have not condemned spontaneous mass revolts, neither have they incited open warfare. Perhaps, in the light of recent events,
Hamilton's "radical reformer" category should be subdi-
vided to distinguish Marxists like the exiled Cleaver from
black nationalists like Stokeley Carmichael. What is most
important, however, is to recognize that, notwithstanding
their revolutionary stance, violent rhetoric and troubles
with the law, such men are *not* terrorists and have not created terrorist organizations. In fact, they stand *between* the
white community and the rage of black youth, perhaps the
last such mediators both sides will enjoy. Should they be
destroyed and should terrorists win the struggle for mass
allegiance, a costly, brutal war of retaliation against the
black community is highly probable.

We noted in Chapter 1 the unusual restraint demonstrated by most white Americans in response to Watts-type
riots. It seems likely that this restraint is linked to the defensive, spontaneous nature of these outbursts, and cannot
be counted on to continue long past the transition from
"self-defense" to what could be termed "aggression."
Aggressive revolts, the reader will recall, helped to justify
the policy of Indian removal by "proving" the unassimilability of the Indians (just as aggressive revolts like Nat

Turner's were used to justify intensified suppression of slaves). Moreover, as Robert W. Tucker has remarked about American attitudes towards external war:

Our position is that whatever grievances a nation may have . . . aggressive warfare is an illegal means for settling those grievances. . . .[7]

. . . Thus, the moral anxiety manifested about the circumstances in which states may legitimately resort to force has its counterpart in the moral complacency shown toward the objectives for which force may be employed against aggression. . . .[8]

Once we feel ourselves the victims of aggression, all restraint vanishes. David Riesman made the same point in a recent magazine article:

As individuals and as a nation we tend to react to attack, or what we define as attack, with unmeasured violence, as we did in the mass bombing of German and Japanese cities, and the demand for unconditional surrender. . . .[9]

This, it seems to me, is the greatest danger now confronting both white men and black men in America, for in outright guerrilla warfare and genocidal counterinsurgency nations lose not only their men but their manhood. Black people would probably lose such a war, but the winners would pay with their souls. This seems too clear to require further argument. It follows that a primary goal of both blacks and whites should be to act so as to make a mass shift towards sympathetic support of guerrillas unnecessary. Without suggesting a detailed plan of action for either community, one can, using this standard, make certain preliminary distinctions between constructive and destructive activity.

What is required, broadly speaking, is decolonization of the ghetto. This implies, of course, a change in the nature of the relationship between black and white America; it implies that legal reforms, integration of the black middle class into white society, "black capitalism," job training, housing projects and better schools are not enough. Decolonization means, first of all, that whites must heed the primary demand of black power advocates. They must evacuate the ghetto, except where there is a clear consensus favoring the retention of white-dominated institutions. What this demand means economically is beginning to be understood; far less attention has been paid to its implications for politics and law enforcement. (For a number of obvious reasons the Kerner Report steered carefully away from making concrete proposals in this area). Leaving these latter implications aside for a moment, we may consider first the demand that ghetto residents be permitted to control their own economies.

Internal control of the ghetto economy suggests, of course, that white-owned commercial enterprises and real estate be turned over to ghetto residents as quickly as possible, and that black workers organize and control their own labor unions or caucuses. On this subject, some black militants and white businessmen are equally glib: private enterprise will do the trick. However, as suggested earlier, the economic failure of the ghetto is attributable not just to race prejudice or personal exploitation but to a breakdown of capitalism under conditions of economic underdevelopment. Strangely enough, the same experts in Washington who admit privately that American-style capitalism may not be the best economic formula for Guinea or Peru think that it is just what the doctor ordered for Harlem and

Watts. And many of the same black leaders who cry out for local autonomy and against "Whitey" welcome the introduction of massive white business enterprises and unions into the ghettos, so long as they create jobs. What this reveals is that no one has yet devised an economic program for the ghetto — capitalist, socialist or any other "ist" — which makes sense. This is not surprising, since we have still not solved the problem of reconciling American aid and investment with the urge to national liberation in less developed nations. Bringing industry into the ghetto may be a good idea; turning ghetto business and properties over to black people may be a good idea, but the question in each case is the same — *how is it to be done, and to what end?* Shall we raise up a new class of black exploiters over the mass of impoverished black consumers? Shall we make entire Negro populations dependent on the beneficence of white industries and white unions for economic advancement? Or are there alternative forms of communal economic enterprise which might work better?

Similarly, consider the alternatives available in the supersensitive area of law enforcement and the administration of justice. Police departments all over the United States are responding to the demand, both from within and without the ghetto, for more efficient law enforcement. In addition, many have been making long overdue moves toward integrating their personnel, ending overt racebaiting and instituting community relations programs. But when it comes to the crucial complaints of ghetto residents — that the police are not "their" police but outsiders unresponsive to their needs and untouched by their grievances, that policemen observe different standards of conduct when dealing with black and white, rich and poor, that they are in effect an army of occupation with a strong propensity of their own for violence — the response has been the organization of police pressure groups. Government officials who propose civilian boards to review citizens' complaints against the police are considered wildly radical; but even civilian boards of review will not end black alienation from the law and its officers. It is time to consider possible solutions which may not seem "politically feasible," but which will give black communities their *own* police forces with administrations elected by and responsible to *them*.

Along the same lines, many Negroes are justifiably alarmed by gun control proposals whose effect will be to disarm *them,* while police departments and National Guard units stock weapons as if World War III were about to be declared. Some militants claim that the possession of arms by ghetto residents is the principal deterrent to greater cruelty, indifference and brutality by police officers assigned to black areas. Whether or not this is true, it seems clear that to discuss respect for law and order, deference to the police and to judicial processes without at the same time taking immediate action to remedy a grossly defective and discriminatory system of law enforcement and criminal justice is both absurd and dangerous. For example, municipal criminal courts are often staffed by political hacks whose chief qualifications are careers as prosecutors and loyalty to anti-Negro political machines. With their overcrowded dockets, overworked employees and antiquated procedures, they are the last places in the world where black men can expect justice. Other nations (the Soviet Union, for example) have devised schemes to bring lower courts closer to the people (the so-called "Comrades' Courts"). It should be possible in the United States to do something more than talk about respect for law and order.

A new effort of imagination is called for, too, when considering governmental efforts to better the lot of ghetto residents. The administration of welfare funds has finally become a national scandal; hopefully, we will soon see the demise of the welfare system and its replacement, perhaps by some form of income maintenance scheme. At the same time, however, one is again compelled to consider the "politically unfeasible." On the local level, one effect of federal welfare programs, including the "war on poverty," has been to strengthen immeasurably the position of existing political machines, now the dispensers of brand-new baskets of goodies. A nice circularity is set in motion, for the revivified machine makes indigenous black political organization more difficult, which increases the probability of riots, which increases the number of programs designed to "stamp out the causes of riots," which are administered — naturally — by the existing machines. All this, because the administration of poverty program funds by independent organizations of the poor is not considered to be "politically feasible." This means, in effect, that Congress has chosen to save political machines while cities burn. Sometimes it seems that we have become a nation of Neros.

One could go on to discuss, in a similar vein, the problems of ghetto education and the move towards community controlled schools, the breakdown of medical and legal services within ghetto walls, and similar topics relevant to the issue of black autonomy and white responsibility. The message, however, should be abundantly clear: it is probably not possible to avert the outbreak of domestic terrorism without the kind of social, political and economic change which makes room in our society for an independent, powerful, decolonized black community. Since more and more proposals for reform are likely to be made in the next few years, it is well to keep in mind that the distinction between constructive and irrelevant or even dangerous proposals has become hard to draw. It is not the same, for example, as the distinction between "brotherhood" and "prejudice." Actions which increase black dependence on white outsiders, reform programs which fail to break the network of vested interests which keeps blacks in a state of colonial subjection, laws which are unenforceable and programs calling for expenditures which legislatures will simply not make are worse than irrelevant; they prove the revolutionaries' contention that talk is a waste of time, and that the system lacks the capacity for radical change. Whether white Americans can end this all-too-American revolt will depend to a large extent on whether they can expand the area of the "politically feasible" to include black decolonization.

Centralism

The real significance of the election in 1968, as several commentators have noted, lay less in Richard Nixon's narrow victory over Hubert Humphrey than in their joint victory — a triumph of what Louis Hartz called "the liberal tradition in America" — over George Wallace. In an election year plagued by civil disorder and assassination the two parties of the Center performed the extraordinary feat of holding the challenges from both Right and Left to less than fifteen percent of the total vote cast. Paradoxically, despite the political divisions created by accelerating social change, Mr. Nixon's victory represented a mandate for continuity rather than for change.

Nixon the campaigner had moved to silence protest from the Right by paying rhetorical obeisance to the theme of "law and order." But with extreme conservatives eliminated (however temporarily) as a politically potent national political force, Nixon the President acted to consoli-

7.

s. Decentralism:
The Deepening Debate

date the liberal Center, pledging to continue federal efforts aimed at the "big three" urban problem areas — jobs, housing and education. His appointment of Daniel P. Moynihan as chief White House Adviser on Urban Affairs was the clearest indication that what might be called "establishment liberalism" was to become the policy of the new administration, at least in the field of domestic policy. A certain subtle shift of emphasis away from the blatant centralism of New Deal Democracy was also apparent in Nixon's announcement of his intention to rely more on private enterprise, in his appointment of Robert Finch to reorganize the Department of Health, Education and Welfare, and in his private negotiations with certain black militants. In fact, the keynote of the new administration might well have been sounded by Moynihan's former colleague at the Harvard-M.I.T. Joint Center for Urban Studies, James Q. Wilson, who suggested that urban police departments should be functionally rather than politically decentralized.[1] Functional decentralization — the devolution of discretionary power downward within an otherwise unchanged central power structure — seemed a likely tack for the new administration to take.

Richard Nixon's victory marked the ending of the first phase in the great debate over urban violence and the beginning of a second. To sum it up rather crudely, the liberal-conservative debate, having been won by the liberals, was now to be succeeded by a liberal-radical struggle whose outcome, as this chapter was written, was very much in doubt. It is important to trace the development of this controversy, for upon its result may hinge the future of America's cities.

The *conservative* position, summarily stated, held that ghetto riots were produced by a combination of explosive material — the black mob or "underclass" consisting of the unemployed, those with criminal records or tendencies and lawless youth — and a spark, the rhetoric of local gang leaders or outside agitators. Reactionaries like George Wallace of Alabama stressed the role of the agitators, seeking to explain their activities as part of a sinister, conspiratorial design to disrupt American society. More sophisticated conservatives emphasized those characteristics of the mob which made them vulnerable to demagoguery and "acting out." For example, the McCone Commission report on the Watts uprising underlined the impatience and "nothing to lose" recklessness of those without a stake in society;[2] other commentators blamed the mass frustration engendered by failure to deliver on liberal promises, or the absence of social controls within the black community produced by centuries of slavery and social disorganization. The common element which justifies labeling these diverse views "conservative" was the assumption that the causes of the violence lay ultimately in the group itself — that ghetto rioting could be attributed to characteristics indigenous and peculiar to certain segments of the urban black community.

The short-term strategies dictated by conservative views were the immediate suppression of actual riots or revolts by the use of *force majeure,* and the avoidance or limitation of potential uprisings by means of police counterinsurgency techniques: surveillance or jailing of agitators, infiltration of gangs and community organizations, the training of specialized riot squads and equipping them with sophisticated antiriot weapons, adoption of preventive detention and high-bail policies intended to keep certain persons off the streets during periods of tension, and so forth. The assumption underlying the strategy of *force majeure* was that black violence, however started, was at bottom expressive rather than instrumental, and that rioters or potential rioters would respond to superior force on the basis of a fairly simple pleasure-pain calculus.

Long-term conservative strategy, however, was more complex. Whether the lumpenproletariat constituted a small minority of the urban black community (as many conservatives believed) or not, its existence as a cause of civil disorder dictated the adoption of economic and political measures designed to eliminate it. One way in which this could be done was to give the rascals a stake in society by providing them with jobs, housing and education. On the other hand, since unfulfilled promises tended to inflame the mob, and since many of the lumpenproles were probably beyond salvation (confirmed criminals, inveterate shirkers, etc.) it was necessary to slow down rather than to accelerate the pace of reform. The dilemma was very much like that faced by counterinsurgency practitioners in Vietnam in their attempt to change South Vietnamese society

145

rapidly enough to provide an alternative to communism while keeping popular expectations "realistically" low. Precisely as in Vietnam, a clear short-term military strategy tended to dominate a vague long-term political strategy. In Chicago as in Saigon, counterinsurgency outweighed reform in the municipal budget for the "hot" season.

Immediately after the Watts uprising, the *liberal* view of urban violence, soon to become the quasi-official governmental interpretation, was also given voice. Critiques of the McCone Commission Report by respected scholars, as well as fresh analysis of later uprisings in other cities, undermined the view that the rioter was a lumpenprole stirred up by lawless despair or outside agitation, emphasizing instead the instrumental nature of civil disorder.[3] The liberal masterwork, the report of the National Advisory Commission on Civil Disorders, found that the rioters were not "criminal types, overactive social deviants, or riffraff" but ordinary blacks born in the city in which the riot took place, economically on a par with their nonrioting neighbors and generally better educated and more politically aware than nonrioters.[4] (Subsequent studies found not only that rioters were "representative" of ghetto communities but that nonrioting members of the community often responded positively to outbreaks of violence in which they did not participate.[5])

The Kerner Report viewed the 1967 outbreaks primarily as a form of protest against the rejection of blacks by American society. It laid very heavy emphasis on patterns of discrimination which kept blacks out of better paying jobs, higher quality housing and competent educational institutions. Noting that, relative to whites, the position of blacks in terms of income, health, education and job employment was worsening rather than improving, it explicitly linked the termination of urban violence to the integration of blacks into the white working and middle classes and elimination of the barriers separating the "two societies." Finally, the report recognized that violence was engendered, in part, by the unresponsiveness of local, white-dominated institutions to black demands for redress of grievances, and offered several suggestions aimed at improving communications between blacks and local governmental agencies.

With respect to short-term solutions to the problem of racial violence, the report's recommendations, like the liberal position in general, varied only slightly from that of the conservatives. It emphasized more effective riot-control training, stricter discipline and command of police and troops in the field, and better planning to avoid disorders or to cut them short after an initial outbreak. The principal departures from the conservative view involved recommending alternatives to deadly force, and the use of community assistance in crisis situations as a way of avoiding escalation of riots. In addition, the report recommended the establishment of intermediary institutions which would open channels of communication between city governments and ghetto residents, for example, neighborhood action task forces, better grievance-response mechanisms, expanded legal services to the poor, and so forth. The combination of short-term recommendations has been described, not inaptly, as a restatement of the philosophy of Theodore Roosevelt: open channels of communication, but carry a big stick.

On a longer-term basis, the liberal strategy for the city, aimed as it was at terminating the "two societies" postulated by the Kerner Report, dictated massive federal efforts to improve the status of blacks relative to whites in the field of jobs, housing and education. This represented a rededication to — rather than an alteration of — political principles espoused by every United States President since Franklin Roosevelt: to wit, that the federal government should take primary responsibility for improving the standard of living of the poor, and ending racial discrimination. The twin principles of governmental centralism and racial integration, which dominated subsequent liberal proposals for reconstruction of the ghetto, shaped the commission's recommendations as well. While advocating large-scale federal programs to solve the unemployment, housing and education problems, the report was vague in recommending measures to increase the collective power of urban blacks at the expense of existing white economic and political interest groups. It therefore contained within itself the seeds of an explosive controversy between centralists and decentralists, integrationists and advocates of black power.

As the first phase in the debate over urban violence and urban strategies was ending in the humiliation of George Wallace, a second phase began. Plans to decentralize the New York school system ended in near bloodshed, a crippling Teachers' Union strike, and the estrangement of New York's Negro and Jewish communities. Indeed, it seemed to some that the consequences of attempted school decentralization verified entirely the principles of strategy defended in Daniel P. Moynihan's *Maximum Feasible Misunderstanding*.[6] There Moynihan had excoriated intellectuals and radicals whose concern for the exercise of political power by the poor — "maximum feasible participation" — had provoked political reprisals causing serious cutbacks in the Democrats' poverty program. Nevertheless, a new and growing school of thought insisted upon the proposition that urban peace could only be achieved, in the long run, by maximizing the power of ghetto dwellers to govern themselves — to control their own schools, police forces, businesses, unions and their own institutions of local government. Like the conservative and liberal strategies, the radical approach reflected a particular view of urban violence — one which emphasized the powerlessness rather than poverty of rioters, and analogized the ghetto uprisings to struggles for national liberation being waged in the Third World. In this view, the chief villain of the piece was not lawlessness, poverty, ignorance or poor housing but a system of interlocking elites operating at the local level through the machinery of urban government to keep blacks in a state of quasi-colonial subjection. The reader is by now familiar with this view. It is time to consider the practical and theoretical objections which have been expressed by liberals in this second phase of debate, and to return again to the question raised in Chapter 4: how, other than by revolution, can an oppressed group accumulate power in a centralized state?

Long-term radical strategy for the city proposes that the ghettos be treated, in certain respects, as cities in themselves: that business enterprises and real property within be turned over to black ownership (preferably by community organizations), that control over ghetto schools be vested in school boards representing ghetto parents, that police forces operating in black territory be made directly responsible to those inhabiting that territory, that the stranglehold of white-dominated political machines over ghetto political life be broken, and that local housing, health, education and welfare programs be administered, whenever possible, by blacks. Each of these proposals, it is recognized, will require serious shifts in the distribution of power in urban areas. Slumlords will be compelled to give up valuable property and businessmen profitable businesses. Urban political machines allied with racketeers will have to abandon a rich vein of political power and graft. An army of welfare workers will be forced to seek other employment and unionized schoolteachers will become responsible to local boards rather than to more acquiescent central authorities. (Little wonder that the Kerner Commission, with its panel of seven politicians, the presidents of a union and a business, a chief of police and a civil rights lawyer, avoided these issues!)

At the same time, radicals believe, federal and state governments must increase their efforts to end poverty, to upgrade schools and housing, to improve urban social services and to end racial discrimination. The apparent inconsistency between this position and the advocacy of black power strategies (which roused the criticism of Mr. Moynihan in *Maximum Feasible Misunderstanding*) deserves comment. Theoretically, the inconsistencies vanish when one recognizes that communities, like nations, may retain their independence while receiving "foreign aid," provided that the aid is consistent with their own development plans. There is no reason why federal aid cannot be given to a community-controlled school or to a community-controlled police force. Similarly, there is no reason — in theory — why the central government should not attempt to create jobs in the ghetto by luring in industry, provided that the relevant unions are entirely open to blacks, and that the industrial development plan has community support. (To increase white power in the ghetto under the guise of reform without simultaneously increasing black power is, as we have seen, an invitation to disaster). On the other hand, the *political* inconsistency between demands for local autonomy and governmental aid remains. How can one drive white landlords out of black communities and then ask the landlords to pay increased taxes to improve ghetto housing? How can one expect white industrialists to locate in areas possessing powerful, black-dominated labor unions, when the same industrialists are moving south in droves to escape strong *white*-dominated unions?

These difficulties cannot be wished away. Urban renewal, which has been a bonanza for white construction industries and unions, may lose their powerful support if black demands for control over urban renewal planning and for a "piece of the action" (through black construction companies and building trades unions) are met. Federal aid to education has had the strong backing of local, state and national teachers' organizations, few of which would be inclined, say, to fight for Rhody McCoy in the Ocean Hill-Brownsville school district of New York. Despite their reported demise, urban political machines proved healthy enough to block the implementation of "maximum feasible participation" by local communities in poverty programs; presumably they are healthy enough to control the local administration of federal aid to the ghettos in 1969–1970. And what of the Average White American? Will he be inclined to foot the tax bill to support black independence in a newly divided city?

No — political reality cannot be wished away. Unfortunately for liberal optimists, however, neither can the desire of the powerless for power and of the dependent for self-rule, which is also a political reality. One is thus confronted with an inescapable strategic choice: to fight for black liberation at the risk of alienating white support for social welfare programs, or to fight for welfare programs at the risk of increasing relative deprivation and further alienating blacks. The radical position is to place primary emphasis on increasing black power at the local level while attempting simultaneously to educate the white public to the need for "foreign aid" to the ghetto. More important, radicals are working to create new political linkways between blacks and other oppressed groups (workers, women, students, and so on) in the hope of creating a coalition which will replace the crumbling liberal alliance in the cities. We explore this in greater detail in the following chapters.

Perhaps the best example of the liberal attack against radical decentralization is a book about the police, *Varieties of Police Behavior,* by Professor James Q. Wilson of Harvard.[7] The following quotations reveal the core of the argument:

For one thing, a central city cannot be fully suburbanized however much we may want to — it is, by definition, central, which means that many people from all over the metropolitan area use it for work, governing and recreation and that, as a result, competing life styles and competing sets of community norms come into frequent and important contact. Necessarily, this generates political pressures to maintain order at the highest level expected by groups who use the city. . . . (p. 288)

Giving central city neighborhoods, many bitterly apprehensive of and hostile toward adjoining neighborhoods, control over their own neighborhood police would be to risk making the police power an instrument for interneighborhood conflict. Proposals for communal police often are based on the tacit assumption that, somehow, only Negroes, and poor Negroes at that, would get control of the police. In fact, legislation that would give the police to Negroes would, out of political necessity, give it to others as well. . . .(pp. 288–89)

. . . if the unit of government becomes the neighborhood . . . the opportunities for a small, self-serving mi-

nority to seize control of the police or the schools will be-
come very great indeed. (*p. 290*)

When the community is deeply divided and emotionally
aroused, the proper governmental policy is not to arm the
disputants and let them settle matters among themselves;
it is, rather, to raise the level at which decisions will be
made to a point sufficiently high so that neither side can
prevail by force majeure *but low enough so that responsi-*
ble authorities must still listen to both sides. (*p. 290*)

Some advocates of communal law enforcement seem in-
clined to defend the model precisely on the grounds that it
avoids the "middle class bias" of the legal code and the
moral order. If by "middle class bias" is meant a concern
for the security of person and property and a desire to
avoid intrusions into one's privacy and disturbances of
one's peace, it is not clear why such concern is a "bias" at
all. . . . (*p. 295*)

Wilson himself recognizes, by mentioning in the same
phrase "control of the police or the schools," that the same
arguments might be directed against any proposal to treat
the ghetto as a political unit, whether for electoral, law-
enforcement, educational or other purposes. It is important to understand, therefore, that they are based on a
series of fallacies which inevitably arise when one attempts
to apply the political philosophy of the New Deal to the
facts of urban life in the 1960's.

The first among these I would call the *fallacy of objec-*
tive order: the doctrine which assumes that since all major
economic classes and ethnic groups in America share certain values — such as "a concern for the security of person and property and a desire to avoid intrusions into
one's privacy and disturbances of one's peace" — there is

a "highest level" of order which may be enforced by a neutral central government. However accurately this consensus theory may describe the various groups which the New Deal attempted to conciliate and order in the 1930's, as applied to the divisions between ghetto dwellers and middle-class whites in present-day cities it is simply untenable. Of course the poor and the rich share certain values, like the desire not to be robbed and murdered. But the existence of such a commonality, in which Fiji Islanders and Albanians also participate, hardly proves the existence of an objective order enforceable in all these communities. Given the necessity of establishing priorities in order to make use of scarce order-maintenance resources, the fact is that black communities and white have different priorities, and therefore different concepts of order.

Like many liberals, Wilson refuses to recognize value differences between domestic groups serious enough to warrant political expression. Those intergroup differences which are acknowledged are treated as evanescent in light of the inevitability of lower-class groups becoming middle-class: "Throughout history the urban poor have disliked and distrusted the police, and the feeling has been reciprocated; the situation will not change until the poor become middle class, or at least working class. . . ." [8] This sounds plausible, but it is not. The Irish poor, for instance, rioted in New York in the 1860's when they had not achieved control over the police or the machinery of city government; a few years later, not much richer, they began to take over both the police department and Tammany Hall, and the "wild Irishman" was no more. Cincinnati's Germans followed the same pattern between 1884 and 1900. Many other domestic groups, as previously noted, resorted to violence in order to gain or protect their control over local government, and to build their particular notions of "law and order" into the legal system, after which violence declined or ceased. Throughout our history, groups seeking embodiment of their group values in governmental form have been compelled to improvise new institutions to do so — the political party, the political machine, the farmers' cooperative, the labor union, the suburb. There is no reason to believe that blacks labor under a necessity any less pressing, or that the existing political system is any more capable of accommodating their demands now than in the past.

Wilson's warning against "making the police power an instrument for interneighborhood conflict" suggests a second fallacy, which I would call *the consensus model of the city*. The warning assumes that the urban police are not now such an instrument, and that through central city government, decisions may be made at "a point sufficiently high so that neither side can prevail by *force majeure* but low enough so that responsible authorities must still listen to both sides." This model describes the operation of no major American city past or present; in fact, it is not even a sensible utopia.

When a city contains within its jurisdiction, as ours have always done, groups differing radically in wealth, power, and degree of political development, the chief purpose served by "raising" the level of decision making is to permit ruling groups to govern through the impersonal machinery of legal bureaucracy — to disguise the exercise of power. As practiced under such circumstances, "coalition government" (including balanced tickets, patronage sharing among groups, etc.) is part of the masquerade, since the representatives appointed for or elected by weak, poverty-stricken, politically unawakened groups are almost inevitably led to serve the interests of the more powerful (or where they do not, they meet the fate of Vito

155

Marcantonio). In short, the interneighborhood conflict which moderates so fear is part and parcel of American urban life. By "raising" the level of decision making to the level, say, of Mayor Yorty's office, or Mayor Daley's, one neighborhood, or set of neighborhoods, is permitted to dominate another so completely that conflict does not seem to exist at all.

As a matter of fact, the fear of conflict runs like a somber thread throughout the work of many urban affairs experts and city planners. Strangely, they seem to prefer the present type of urban government, in which conflict is ignored or "managed" in totalitarian fashion, to one in which very real differences between large racial and economic groups would be embodied in systematic form. I say "strangely" because institutionalization of political differences seems a likely way to lessen rather than to increase violent conflict. For example, if governmental power were to devolve downward to the black, Spanish-American or Appalachian ghettos, meaningful bargaining and coalition government would then become a possibility, since only then would the poor have something to bargain with. Similarly, although "making the police power an instrument for interneighborhood conflict" may seem a frightening prospect to some, to the residents of various ghettos the police are already the principal instrument of interneighborhood conflict (disguised as a conflict between law enforcers and lawbreakers). It is for this reason that they feel constrained to support the activities of antipolice neighborhood organizations, citizens patrols and political organizations like the Black Panther party.

In this respect, it is particularly important to emphasize that blacks seeking local power want what whites, whether in urban or suburban areas, already possess. Wilson's third fallacy is *the false black-white analogy* — the notion that

156

the present structure of urban government seriously limits white power, and that the extension of community control principles to the white community will therefore lead to weakening the position of minorities. ("In fact, legislation that would give the police to Negroes would, out of political necessity, give it to others as well. . . .") In the first place, a downward devolution of power *within* the majority community need not occur if whites are satisfied with the extent to which the institutions of local government now respond to their demands and desires. For example, it is perfectly possible to imagine Harlem or Bedford-Stuyvesant with its own police force (or, for that matter, with its own mayor) without the Bronx feeling it necessary to secede from Queens or Staten Island. This is because those middle-class groups which have sought community control of local institutions have obtained it, or can obtain it on demand.

When white parents remove their children from urban public schools and send them to private and parochial schools, this is not called "community control" and produces little conflict. When whites move to the suburbs, whose governmental institutions are responsive not only to demands but to whims, this does not create great political issues or generate strikes. And although urban groups like the Jews of New York, the Poles of Chicago, the Irish of Boston, and the WASPs of Dallas clearly control not just their own schools or police forces but segments of industry and the professions, labor unions, churches, networks of fraternal and voluntary organizations, rackets and political organizations, these groups have all successfully opposed community power for others. It would be difficult to show how the present structure of urban government constrains such groups or limits their power locally. Nevertheless, in those cases in which whites do not enjoy self-government it is hardly proper to subject them to oppression on the grounds that they might misuse their power, or that they are "racist." Community control is not intended to repeal the United States Constitution.

The final fallacy which deserves comment is contained in the statement that, with community control a reality, "the opportunities for a small, self-serving minority to seize control of the police or the schools will become very great indeed. . . ." This is a familiar colonialist argument — the same, in fact, which was directed by Great Britain against the independence of the American colonies and India, by France against the independence of Algeria and her other colonies, and by the American South against the independence of the slaves. As applied to local government in the United States, it is based on an outmoded reading of history which assumes that "that government is best which governs most," and that the worst thing one can do is to permit the government to get too close to the people. For example, Wilson states: "If the study of urban politics has taught us anything, it is that, except on referenda, and perhaps not even then, 'the people' do not govern — organizations, parties, factions, politicians, and groups govern. . . ." [9]

Is it so easy to destroy all distinction between elitism and democracy? In the real world, I would have thought, one could attempt in a rough way to rank various governmental types and arrangements along a continuum leading, let us say, from the relative elitism of Saudi Arabia to the relative democracy of Sweden. However, the quoted statement simply begs the question. If indeed "groups govern," the question remains whether it is possible and advisable for specific groups to govern themselves, or to be governed by indigenous rather than exogenous subgroups. And the question suggests an answer: it is the state of political development of the group governed as much as the form of government which decides the extent to which "the people" govern, either directly or indirectly. In practice this means that one simply cannot "prefer" central governmental power to local power, or vice versa, as a matter of principle for all time. Under some circumstances, maximizing human freedom may require that the central government assume vast new powers in order to counterbalance increased private power; in others it will require that oppressed and alienated communities become self-determining. The argument between Hamilton and Jefferson is unending precisely because the source of unfreedom shifts over time. At the moment its focus lies in the coalition of white interests dominating urban governments.

The fear of the small, pernicious minority which will take power in a communal government in order to oppress the community is a phobia generated by certain specific traumas. In the last century the chief advocates of strong local government were either southerners, to whom "states' rights" meant white rights, or industrialists, to whom "freedom of persons" meant freedom of corporations to ride roughshod over workers and consumers. From 1880 to 1930 "strong city government" meant rule by machine bosses and their myrmidons over the hapless, malleable immigrant masses. Strong local government under conditions of political somnolence means that power will be grabbed by those piratical enough to grab it and utilized by those ruthless enough to utilize it. However, under conditions in which the governed are awakening to their collective identity, history, suffering and rights, the situation is reversed, and the traumatic precedents mentioned above do not bind. Others, more relevant to the case at hand, come to mind: local government after the Jeffersonian revolution, when state legislatures and town meetings struck down property qualifications for voting and religious tests, established state universities and began, for the first time, to reflect the demands of the "little man"; state legislatures in the South under Reconstruction, which pioneered in social legislation and racial reform; state and local legislatures under Populist rule, which sixty years before the New Deal attempted to regulate industry and to control the quality of food sold to the public; cities under Socialist or Progressive mayors early in the present century, which initiated modern city planning and "good government," and certain state legislatures in the 1920's and 1930's which attempted to secure the rights of labor and to legislate for the poor.

The argument against political decentralization and community control, therefore, seems to me to rest on a series of fallacies — elaborate rationalizations, really, for preserving the status quo and the hegemony of the Center. This leaves us, however, with the dilemma described earlier and restated by Moynihan's argument from political infeasibility: with power both at local and federal levels in the hands of the same interlocking elites, how can an outgroup gain sufficient collective power to enter into the bargaining process? In the next and final chapter, we consider the problem of revolution in the United States.

Rev

*L*ogic compels us, finally, to consider the question of revolution. For if the solution to the problem of group revolt is a social and political transformation which admits the powerless to power, we have already begun to talk about a kind of revolution. And if the period of transformation has, in fact, begun, it is necessary to inquire into its nature and to speculate about its probable outcome. The discussion will be brief and, of necessity, speculative; we are too close to the subject to claim objectivity. Nevertheless, it is at precisely such times that historical perspective is needed. Does the social and political disorder of the 1960's betoken a subsequent period of even greater disorder and more rapid change? Are we living in a prerevolutionary era? The answer depends to a large extent upon one's perspective on the American past.

First, however, we must grapple with a loaded word: "revolution." When historians say (as they so often do)

ution in America

that the United States has never experienced a revolution, we are entitled to know what they mean. For example, Barrington Moore believes that the American struggle for independence was *not* a true revolution because it was not accompanied by significant social change; the bourgeoisie, which had run the prerevolutionary show, continued to run it after 1781.[1] J. Franklin Jameson and other historians think that it *was* a revolution because it *was* accompanied by genuine social change — the elimination of a domestic aristocracy and a transfer of power to small businessmen, artisans and farmers.[2] Charles Beard thought that it started out to be a revolution but was undone by the reaction of 1789;[3] whereas Hannah Arendt believes that it *was* a true revolution although *not* accompanied by genuine social change, since the struggle brought into the world a brand-new type of constitutional democracy.[4] Similarly, when social scientists or political figures state, as is their wont, that revolution in the United States is impossible, again we are entitled to know what they mean. According to Charles Beard, the Civil War was a revolution; does the statement then mean that civil war in the United States is now impossible? According to Arthur Schlesinger, Jr., the ages of Jackson and Roosevelt were revolutionary times; are we to conclude that further political transformations are now impossible in America?

Superficially, the problem is one of evidence, but only superficially. It is true that dispute continues about the facts of the American Revolution, the age of Jackson, the Civil War and the New Deal — Was there really a Tory "aristocracy"? Did small farmers really exercise power under Jackson? — the disagreements among the authorities noted above would not disappear even if all of them accepted the same facts. Moore, for example, could still hold that transfer of power from large to petit bourgeois is not a revolution (and perhaps not even a power transfer), and Arendt still assert that whether or not the colonial bourgeoisie maintained their position is irrelevant in the light of the political significance of the American Revolution. Perhaps, then, the problem is one of definition; Hannah Arendt suggests as much when she states that one ought to distinguish French-style social revolutions from American-style political ones (and, one might now add, from Algerian- or Vietnamese-style wars of national liberation). But such definitional disputes are only symptoms of a more profound disagreement. At issue is the fundamental question: "What kind of change makes a difference?" Amid the welter of political changes that characterize any rapidly developing society, which changes alter the political system so rapidly, drastically and permanently as to be called revolutionary?

Note that this question itself implies a definition, but it

is a definition based upon what political analysts seem to mean when they use the word — that is, change occurring over a fairly short period of time (in any event, not more than fifteen years or so) which replaces an "old" political system (not just a regime) with a "new" one which lasts for a while. Like all definitions, this one begs substantive questions — What is meant by "political system"? How does one tell when a "new" system has come into existence? All I want to do here, however, is to establish some principles of exclusion and clarification. We are *not* concerned with evolutionary change, although we will come back to the evolutionist posture, common among American scholars, which assumes that revolutionary change in the United States is a fiction. Nor are we concerned with nonpolitical "revolutions," such as those in science and technology, except as they affect politics. Finally, we do not adopt as a matter of definition the concept of revolution as inevitably violent, but leave the relationship of violence to revolution for later formulation. With this by way of background, *has* America ever experienced a revolution?

To begin with, it is clear that America has not had a proletarian revolution in the Marxist sense. In Marxist terms the United States remains at present, as it has always been, a bourgeois society characterized by private ownership and control of the means of production and distribution, minimal government regulation of business, trade unions dedicated to strengthening rather than replacing the capitalist system, individual rather than collective farming, and so forth. Many factors have been advanced to explain the nonoccurrence of a revolution of the proletariat, among them the absence of a feudal aristocracy to set the Marxist dialectic in motion, the availability of cheap land as a safety valve, America's incredible affluence, and the ability of the capitalist class to save itself periodically via reforms, co-optation of dissidents and destruction of radical movements. All these factors help to explain what did *not* happen. As a springboard for discussion of what *did* happen to change the American political system between 1776 and 1969 an idea of Richard Hofstadter's may be more useful: in America, he states, "ethnic animosities . . . have been at times almost a substitute for the class struggle." [5]

America does lack a revolutionary tradition in the Marxist sense, but she has, as we have seen, experienced revolts aplenty, from Indian and slave rebellions, farmer revolts and nativist terrorism through labor-management warfare, race rioting and the ghetto revolts and campus confrontations of the present time. We have pointed out that many rebellious out-groups have been homogeneous "subnations"; that their rebellious actions have been aimed at redeeming their territory, jobs and lives from control by outsiders; that the dynamics of internal colonialism generates such movements for group liberation; and that those in authority have often responded to such revolts ineffectually rather than participating in the system transformation required to satisfy the demands of large excluded groups. The existence of this tradition of group insurrection strengthens Hofstadter's thesis by demonstrating that group consciousness in America supersedes, or prevents, the development of class consciousness. But if this is so, perhaps we have been looking for the wrong sort of revolution in American history. Perhaps domestic revolution is merely revolt writ large.

Generally, movements which begin as revolts end as revolts. A group which comes to conceive of itself as an oppressed nation or subnation distinguishes itself, in the process, from those who are outsiders and tends to move in the direction of local autonomy or independence rather than seizure of central power. For this reason, although such movements are often *locally* revolutionary, they seem profoundly nonrevolutionary with regard to the political system as a whole. On the other hand, in at least three situations, insurrectionary movements may become revolutionary in the sense that they require a rapid transformation of the entire system:

(1) When those defining themselves as a group are so numerous, in control of such a large geographical area, and so nation-conscious as to attempt secession with some hope of success.

(2) When a single group excluded from power at all levels attempts to force a system transformation by resort to "aggressive" violence. (Since the group may be threatened with extinction, such violence is not necessarily "aggression"; the term is used here to describe attacks outside rebel territory.)

(3) When similarly situated groups conducting separate revolts join forces for the purpose of gaining power simultaneously through radical change in the political system.

The best-known instances of revolutionary secessionism are, of course, the American Revolution and the southern rebellion which precipitated the Civil War. (Many Indian revolts may also fall into this category, since they aimed at independent control of large geographical areas, but most tribes found collaboration for the purpose of joint rebellion impossible.) A key to the development of major secessionist movements is the growth of nation-consciousness among groups which may be extremely diverse economically, politically and even culturally. Those who came to consider themselves "Americans" began as Virginia planters or Boston traders; to a great extent, the unifying group definition which they eventually adopted was forced upon them by British mercantilists. Similarly, "Southerners" originally owing primary loyalty to a state or class were driven together by northern attacks upon all classes of white southerners simultaneously. Such movements have been revolutionary in effect rather than in intention, for no matter what form of government the secessionists adopted, the effect of the separation itself would be to alter the original system immediately and profoundly. Imagine the northern United States confronted on its southern border by an expansionist slave power ambitious to conquer Central and South America — a North without a southern investment outlet, deprived of half of the free land of the West, forced to trade as a foreign nation for cotton, oil, natural gas and other southern products — and the revolutionary implications of southern secession become apparent.

At present there exists only one serious domestic secessionist movement: the movement to establish an independent black state somewhere within the continental United States (probably within the South, where selective Negro immigration might make it possible to gain legal control of certain states). As white oppression of all black economic and social classes simultaneously continues to generate black nationalism, independence sentiment appears to be gaining substantial support among northern ghetto dwellers. The movement deserves more serious study than it has so far received, particularly since the most "obvious" objections — that the numbers of people involved are too small, that the new nation could not support itself economically or that "it could never happen" — prove on analysis to be unfounded. Like white nationalism in the South after 1865, black nationalism is not revolutionary in effect except as to the territory claimed. It is therefore possible to imagine the United States government several years and major riots hence permitting a black state to become independent (at least with regard to domestic affairs) as a way of ridding the nation of an "insoluble" problem. The more cogent objection is not that such a development is impossible, but that it is probably fruitless, since the fate of small neighbors of the United States is to be dominated either by the United States or some countervailing foreign power. The use of local power bases to forge, with other dissident groups, a new domestic alliance would seem to be better designed to maximize black power.

Black nationalism could become revolutionary, however, whether or not secession were a goal, under the circumstances described in category 2. Continued exclusion from collective power at all levels produces widespread fear of permanent exclusion and ultimate group extinction. Under the circumstances, from the point of view of the excluded group, terrorism directed against "the enemy" wherever he may be found is justifiable self-defense; the fact that massive counterforce may destroy the group is no deterrent, since the rebels prefer a brave death to perpetual dependence and the elimination of their militant members. The United States has not experienced this type of revolution before, for at least two reasons. First, the nation has never before been so centralized and so integrated (politically and economically) as to permit the members of a ruling coalition to collaborate in maintaining power at all levels. Earlier insurgent groups found it possible to take power locally; later groups benefited from the growth of federal power under the New Deal and its successors; present-day blacks find both roads blocked, except where they constitute a majority or near majority in the cities. (Even here, there is talk of instituting "metropolitan-regional governments" which would operate to nullify such black majorities.) Second, never before has the excluded group been a caste with revolutionary-national potential. (For reasons which have been previously explored, less cohesive groups with a shorter history of oppression have lacked this potential.) As a result, failing a radical redistribution of power under her present political system, America must face the prospect of a new type of domestic revolutionary movement which would seek to generate the necessary transformation by force.

It is very difficult, of course, to identify outright revolutionaries presently active within or without the ghetto, or to measure the extent of such activity or the degree to which it commands mass support. Even criminal convictions, such as those obtained against members of the Revolutionary Action Movement for conspiracy to assassinate certain political leaders, indicate little about the nature and extent of revolutionary activity; the possibility of frame-ups in such cases is greater than usual. What seems clear, however, is that there *are* organizations with some standing in the black community which will initiate revolutionary activity if the situation deteriorates further — for example, if the police are "unleashed" upon ghetto activists, or if there is an attempt at forced relocation of the black population. The largest and best organized of these is the Black Panther party, with establishments in half a dozen cities or more. Despite occasional shoot-outs with police, the imprisonment of West Coast leader Huey Newton, and the exile (to escape imprisonment) of Minister of Information Eldridge Cleaver, the Panthers are not yet revolutionary activists. Along with other street organizations (for example, certain of the large gangs in New York, Chicago, Detroit and Los Angeles), they stand in the wings of the revolutionary theater, waiting to enter if whites decide upon the forcible suppression of black militancy. A dangerous game? Certainly. But, to many blacks, no more dangerous than waiting passively for the blow to fall.

If the United States is now entering a revolutionary period, racial conflict alone, however, will not explain what is happening to the present political system. For this purpose we must consider a more characteristic type of revolutionary movement in America — the alliance of militant out-groups with dissidents in power which radically alters both the distribution of power and its mode of exercise throughout the system. Three examples of such alliance come to mind: the Jeffersonian, which isolated New England business interests, brought the two-party system into existence and the "little man" into the electoral process, and opened up the West for mass settlement; the northern Republican, which joined eastern businessmen and "native" workers with western farmers and abolitionists on a new ethnic-sectional basis, unleashed the energies of northern capitalism and doomed the slave system to violent extinction; and the New Deal, which joined organized workers, immigrant groups, farmers and elements of the business community in a new coalition, expanded the federal government beyond the Founding Fathers' wildest dreams, and created a mixed economy and a welfare-warfare state. None of these alliances was revolutionary in the sense that capitalist power was destroyed: each contained important elements of the business and commercial communities while attacking others. None came to power by formally overthrowing a preexisting political system, although in each case the opposition claimed that the methods used to take and exercise power (e.g., creation of political parties, expansion of presidential power, election by a minority of a sectional party candidate, expansion of federal government) were illegitimate. Similarly, none succeeded by force of arms alone, although, as will be explained in a moment, violence played an important role in each case. In what sense, then, were these alliances "revolutionary"?

The difficulty is that we are accustomed to thinking about political systems on the basis of two contrasting models: the *revolutionary model,* in which a society characterized by rigid class distinction, extremist ideologies and a suppressive political apparatus is ripped apart from time to time, and the *evolutionary model,* in which a liberal economic-political apparatus permits free play among interest groups in an essentially classless society, thus making possible change which is peaceful and gradual rather than violent and sudden. (A further implication in the contrast is that change in the revolutionary society is cyclical, and ultimately to no avail, while change in the evolutionary society is linear, and therefore "progressive.") Americans who deny that their nation has experienced a revolution generally have in mind images drawn from the experiences of revolutionary societies: the *canaille* have never stormed the White House; the Bolsheviks have never subverted the army; America has never passed an election nor General Motors a dividend; therefore, there has been no revolution. But the distinction between revolutionary and evolutionary societies is a gross exaggeration, if not entirely false. France, the Soviet Union and China have known peaceful change and progress, while many of the most significant alterations of the American political system have been revolutionary in character. That is, drastic alterations both in the distribution of power and the mode of exercising it have been made rapidly, extralegally and — in a sense now to be explained — violently.

Consider two contrasting scenarios. (A) Armed peasants

surround the palace. Their leader breaks into the throne room, kills the king and promulgates a new constitution. This we call a "violent revolution." (B) Armed peasants surround the palace. Their leader is granted an audience with the king. The king counts up the number of peasants and the number of his troops and promulgates an amended constitution. This we call "peaceful change."

Facetious though it may be, scene B comes closer to the truth about political change in the United States than does the theory of peaceful evolution. Despite the fact that in America group consciousness has often superseded class consciousness, major alterations of the political order have taken place against a background of civil disorder and potential revolution or civil war. The admission of new group alliances to power has been accomplished through redefinition of the system itself, involving both the improvisation of new institutions and the exercise of powers formerly held to be unconstitutional. And new alliances, with their new constitutions, have frequently consolidated their power violently. These principles are illustrated by the three movements described above.

Jeffersonian. Jefferson and his new party came to power at the conclusion of two decades of farmer uprisings and urban riots, after a serious attempt at counter-revolution had been made by the ruling Federalists. Naturally enough, the Federalists considered the idea of competitive political parties to be seditious and unconstitutional, especially since Jefferson himself was a self-declared French sympathizer and revolutionary. If the Alien and Sedition Acts, which filled the jails with political prisoners, had not been repealed and Jefferson elected in 1800, the farmer-planter-worker coalition would either have become an armed alliance (Jeffersonians had been active among the Whiskey Rebels and were prepared to "nullify" offensive legislation) or the West would have attempted to secede (up to the time of the Louisiana Purchase, such attempts were still being made). Jefferson's presidency was considered by the great John Marshall to be a series of attacks on the United States Constitution, and Federalist New England continued to plot against the "Antichrist" in office until Jeffersonians fomented a war with England and Canada. The war ruined New England shipping, drove that section to threaten secession, and utterly destroyed the Federalist party. So complete was Jefferson's triumph that the two-party system became thereafter a one-party system, until Andrew Jackson attacked the Bank of the United States and regenerated an organized opposition.

Northern Republican. The northern Republican alliance was forged in an era of national disintegration, as civil disorder rose in the 1850's toward the level of civil war. The Republican party itself was founded in the year the Kansas-Nebraska civil war began; six subsequent years of violence polarized proslave and antislave sentiment North and South, driving the Whig party into the Republican coalition and splitting the Democratic party in two. As in the case of the Jeffersonian revolution, the law (in the form of Supreme Court interpretations of the Constitution) clearly favored the *ancien régime,* while congressional legislation in the 1850's reflected the conservative views of Stephen Douglas. The election of Lincoln — a minority President — deprived the system of its last ounce of legitimacy from the southern point of view, and the bloodiest war of the nineteenth century commenced. Civil disorder continued in the North throughout Lincoln's first administration (the New York draft riot was but the most serious of numerous anti-Republican riots and disturbances), and the Republicans would probably not have remained in power in 1864

but for the dubious soldiers' vote and the absence of southern voters. In fact, as Milton Viorst has suggested, Republican power rested for a long time on sheer force:

*Relying on a minority faction as their base of support, the
Republicans never quite managed to find a majority that
was consistent and reliable. In 1868 and 1872, Grant won
respectively by 300,000 and 750,000 votes, but in both
elections virtually all of the white voters of the South were
disfranchised. In 1876 and 1888, the Republican candidate
actually polled fewer popular votes than the Democratic
while achieving victory in the electoral college. . . .
Thus, of seven elections from 1868 to 1892, the Republicans won five, but in only one — Benjamin Harrison's
narrow victory in 1888 — could they claim a nationwide
majority.*[6]

Thus for a second time a revolutionary coalition was
formed against the backdrop of civil disorder, and went to
war to consolidate its gains, ruling a virtually one-party
state for a long while thereafter.

New Deal. In the mid-1930's, with homeless farmers
afoot and workers fighting bloody battles on the picket
line, domestic fascists and Communists gaining broad support and the nation filled with a fear of violent revolution,
Franklin Roosevelt made his famous "left turn" and rode
to triumph on the shoulders of a new coalition. Again, the
new alliance exercised power through instrumentalities
which seemed both un-American and illegal, and which
were for a long time held to be so by the United States
Supreme Court. Again, changes in the political system
were rapid and profound. And again, although Roosevelt
can hardly be said to have "fomented" World War II, it
was war, rather than politics as usual, which silenced the

domestic opposition, solved the problems of unemployment and underproduction, and made possible Roosevelt's four terms. Postwar militarization and prosperity ensured the continuing hegemony of the coalition which ruled through both political parties without serious challenge until civil disorder began anew in the 1960's.

Perhaps these movements were not revolutionary in the Marxist sense. Very well, but the moral is clear: how much civil disorder there has been, how much turmoil, and how much blood spilled just to obtain the relatively minor structural changes represented by the alliances of Jefferson, Lincoln and Roosevelt!

We have drawn attention to modern manifestations among black Americans of secessionism and violent revolt, and have noted that such movements are not at present revolutionary, although their revolutionary potential increases with the passage of time and the continuation of black powerlessness. The matter of revolutionary alliances, however, generates additional questions for the contemporary analyst. Is the period of mass protest and civil disorder which began earlier in the 1960's the modern equivalent of the 1790's, 1850's or 1930's? Against the backdrop of this disorder, is a new political alliance in the process of formation? If so, will it take power nonviolently or resort to violence? In either case, will there be the equivalent of a counterrevolution? Obviously, when one is deeply involved in the events of the day, answers to such questions come hard. Nevertheless, it is worthwhile to speculate on the possible persistence of the pattern elucidated thus far.

As mentioned earlier, one factor inhibiting mass revolutionary movements in the United States has been the inclination of oppressed groups sharing a common cultural heritage to define themselves as "nations," thus making it initially very difficult to work with "outsiders." On the other hand, we have also seen that prolonged revolt can produce a political awakening in which the insurgent group, increasingly aware of its goals and impatient for power, seeks like-minded allies from without. The result, therefore, is a three-stage process, through which several domestic groups are now proceeding: (a) cooperation with a broad cross-section of similarly situated groups and groups in power for purposes of gaining quick access to the system through moderate reform; (b) disillusionment and withdrawal from multigroup activity, selection of new leaders, redefinition of goals and solidification on the basis of group nationalism; and (c) cooperation with carefully selected groups in and out of power as part of a broader strategy for radical change.

It is interesting to note, in this regard, that it is now the most militant black leaders who speak of a black-white alliance — men like the late Malcolm X and Eldridge Cleaver — while orthodox black nationalists appear to have reached a plateau in terms of both their numbers and their political thought. Equally important, black students, both in high schools and in colleges, have established patterns of cooperation with members of other minority groups as well as white radicals. Meanwhile, the latter move through the same three-stage process, beginning with indiscriminate collaboration (as in the civil rights movement and Senator Eugene McCarthy's presidential campaign in 1968), continuing into withdrawal and the development of group nationalism (as we shall see in a moment, this is happening right now) and ending in selective collaboration based upon a redefined group interest.

Implicit in the idea of revolutionary group alliances rather than economic class alliances is the notion that the unit of revolt in America is the "subnation," and that before there can be an alliance there must be conscious and coherent subnational groups. This is why it is so difficult at present to plot the development of new alliances; not all potential members have yet experienced the process described above. For white radicals, for example, the question is whether their group identity will be stabilized and maintained beyond college, and after termination of the Vietnam War. Young radicals clearly do *not* fit easily into the tradition of group insurgency represented by Appalachian farmers, white southerners and urban blacks, since in one sense they are not a "subnation"; and in another, being predominantly middle-class in origin, they are not an out-group at all. In an almost Darwinian response to these requirements, however, they are in the process of creating an *ethos* — an amalgam of cultural tastes, political attitudes, ethical norms and social mores which is the analogue of ethnicity, or perhaps even a new form of it. (One piece of evidence supporting this thesis is the growth of a racist stereotype which pictures all radicals as dirty, oversexed, foul-smelling, addicted to drugs, incurably violence-prone, etc. — in fact the whole battery of anti-Irish and anti-Negro prejudices!) Additionally, as they emerge from college without returning to the family fold or entering the world of the great corporations and traditional professions, their movement develops an economic base comprising selected traditional occupations (such as teaching or labor union work), newly created occupations (community organizing, international development work and service in independent institutes or foundations), and new branches of traditional occupations (legal services for the poor, group medical practice, community-owned businesses).

Additionally, like their rebellious predecessors, today's new leftists seek the equivalent of controllable territory by occupying existing communities (the East Village in New

York, Old Town in Chicago or the Telegraph area of Berkeley), participating in community control movements elsewhere and attempting to play a more authoritative role in the administration of universities and university communities. Violent confrontations on college campuses become somewhat more comprehensible when one keeps in mind that the student activists and their supporters are not merely reformers attempting to improve their lot during a four-year hitch, or young folks raising youthful hell. They are members of an emerging social and political group with hopes of permanence, whose principal economic, political and territorial base is, and will remain for some time the university community. Those colleges which have experienced the most intense conflict have therefore been precisely those in cities in which a radical community is in the process of formation both on and off campus. It comes as no surprise to see the most explosive confrontations taking place in San Francisco, Boston, New York and Chicago.

As the pace of political change quickens, other outgroups are experiencing a process of revolt and awakening similar to that undergone by urban blacks and white radicals. In some cases, the process is telescoped into a comparatively short period of time; the militant organization of labor leader Cesar Chavez, for example, has had an electrifying effect on the Mexican-American farm workers of California. Mexican Americans in the Southwest have begun to fight for their lost land. A new cadre of American Indian leaders now preaches the doctrine of "red power" to willing ears, and at several universities American Indian students have joined black and African, Asian and Latin American "Third World" students in confrontations with police. In other cases, the initial period of collaboration has barely begun. Despite awakening outside interest in the rural poor and their unemployed brethren in the cities, the masses of rural poor people and poor urban whites remain voiceless. Yet even here there are signs of stirring — the "black lung" revolt of West Virginia miners, the participation of Appalachian whites and Puerto Ricans in the Poor People's March of 1968, the formation of community unions among urban "hillbillies," and so forth.

The formation of a new out-group alliance with revolutionary political potential has therefore not yet occurred. It would be rash, however, to predict that it could not occur in a fairly short time — say by 1975 — given the speed of the spreading wave of political awakening. Before this can take place, the historical material suggests that one other change is necessary: a falling out among members of the present ruling coalition. In the past, no significant alteration of the political system has occurred without the development of serious divisions among groups in power; all past alliances which have been successful have split the middle and upper middle classes, attaching elements of each to the new coalition. This, of course, is one reason why American revolutionary movements do not seem "revolutionary," and why some radicals now argue that the new alliance, if any, must be anticapitalist. In any event, it is fairly clear that the disintegration of the present ruling coalition has already begun. The development of a radical group identity among large elements of the young has already split the suburban middle class, at least generationally. Furthermore, organized labor is now entering a period characterized by widespread discontent with the established leadership, political polarization and competition between dissidents of the Right and the Left, and the growth of schismatic movements at both local and national levels.

The fact that in 1968 the established union leadership

kept the labor vote generally in line for Hubert Humphrey was widely misinterpreted as a sign that no significant changes were taking place in that movement. Political scientists have an unfortunate tendency to interpret electoral behavior as the key to a group's politics when, for a variety of reasons, how men vote may bear little relationship to their deepest political desires and clearest intentions. For example, probably labor voted for Humphrey not because the rank and file trusted George Meany or shared his political philosophy, but because there was no viable candidate of the Right (George Wallace being a southerner with a lifelong record of opposition to labor) or the Left (Robert Kennedy being dead, and the other candidates of the Left black socialists) to whom they could turn. The vote for Nixon-Humphrey, the candidates of the Center, may have represented a widely felt wish for peace and order — but, as we have seen, such wishes are by no means inconsistent with action at the group level whose effect is to overthrow the established order. In any event, developments since that election — including a formal schism between the conservative AFL-CIO and the more liberal United Auto Workers and Teamsters Unions, the formation of radical and black caucuses in dozens of labor unions, the organization of white block clubs and "support your local police" associations in many blue-collar neighborhoods, and the formation of new unions, both right-wing and left-wing, outside the established labor structure — make it clear that the processes of change within the labor movement are accelerating rather than slowing down.

The very same thing is true (although not often recognized by radical critics of the establishment) of other traditionally capitalist or managerial groups, many of which are in the process of being "declassed" as the result of a growing socioeconomic gap between lower middle and upper middle classes. As the technological revolution proceeds and industrial concentration continues, as costs of living and of doing business rise without letup, Horatio Alger begins to disappear even as myth. Small businessmen know that they will never be big businessmen; they will be lucky to be able to educate their children. Small farmers know that their days on the land are numbered, and that the only successful farmer is the agricultural corporation. Even within the corporate world, lower management personnel are aware that they have "plateaued out" — and that survival rather than advancement is now the goal. As John McDermott has pointed out, lower management jobs, like those of teachers and many professionals, are being industrialized.[7] All of these groups and more (including a growing proportion of younger professionals and intellectuals) have common complaints based in part upon the powerlessness and boredom of life in a technocratic society. And it may be that they will discover they have common enemies. When this happens, a revolutionary alliance will be in existence.

At this point, however, one must confront directly a question which plagues any analyst of contemporary social change, particularly if his sympathies are with the dispossessed. We have seen on several occasions that although working-class and middle-class discontent may catalyze a revolutionary alliance, it may also be directed socially downward, against those out-groups which are in direct competition for jobs and living space with workers and members of the lower middle class. The specter of domestic reaction — the formation, out of the wreckage of the present political system, of a right-wing alliance which would annihilate moderates and radicals alike — is frequently invoked in these troubled days to prevent those out of power from "rocking the boat."

"If you think what you have now is bad, just wait until your real enemies take over!" runs the refrain. American radicals are frequently reminded that the German Communists of the early 1930's helped to bring Hitler to power by voting with the Nazis in the Reichstag in order to weaken the ruling Social Democratic coalition. In effect, defenders of the status quo contend that, as in Germany in 1931–1932, the only alternative to rule by the present coalition in the United States is a police state — an argument which rests upon the assumption that what most workers, small businessmen, farmers, housewives and professionals really want is an authoritarian government which would establish order at all costs. Therefore, the argument concludes, increasing political agitation, which produces social disorder, is the surest road to domestic fascism.

To this line of reasoning there is no easy answer. The possibility of a realignment dominated by a right-wing coalition is one of the risks to be weighed by any group which seeks to alter the distribution of political power. One would be worse than a fool to adopt the slogan of the German Communists, "After the Nazis, us," as an article of faith or a corollary of historical necessity. There is, however, a more complex and persuasive answer.

It is erroneous to assume that what any group "really" wants is either stability *or* change; most groups want both simultaneously. By measuring reactions and testing group responses at a time when existing political configurations are beginning to break up — at an early stage in the process of political polarization and alliance formation — one will almost always find a vast majority of those polled leaning towards stability. There are several reasons for this: the inevitability of change is not yet accepted; initial reactions to conduct which seems unusual and "disorderly" are usually negative; and since new alliances are not yet formed, each group desires change for itself and stability for everyone else. Thus, at the beginning of what we might call the revolutionary process, the Right always seems extremely strong. As the process continues, however, initial reactions to social disorder are qualified (this may be seen, for example, by comparing the results of polls of urban blacks taken immediately after ghetto riots with those taken somewhat later). The society becomes conditioned to accepting a higher degree of political militancy and social turbulence (compare the front-page newspaper coverage of the 1964 disturbance at Berkeley with the minimal reporting of the much more serious People's Park disturbance of 1969). The irreversibility of change is increasingly accepted, and the question is then not *whether* there will be change or order but what *kind* of change will prevail. At this point, diverse groups realize that they cannot fight alone, new alliances are formed, and eventually a new national consensus may come into being.

This analysis does not tell us very much about the shape and content of the new consensus; it does not, for example, negate the possibility of domination by the extreme Right. What it *does* show, however, is that sampling public opinion prematurely is not only useless but misleading, particularly where such samples are used to predict the probable outcome of a period of revolutionary change. If a rightist coalition eventually takes power, it will not be composed of sentimental opponents of change but of the apostles of a new order — for example, overt racists and militarists. But the ultimate Right is no more identifiable at present than the ultimate Left. No group in American society is inherently "right-wing" or "left-wing," especially since the meaning of these terms continues to change. The shape of the future political system therefore depends upon how the groups we have discussed come to perceive their interests as the revolutionary process continues — whom they deem to be their friends and whom their enemies.

Will the labor movement five to ten years hence follow the successors of George Wallace or the successors of Robert Kennedy? Will members of the lower middle class support existing business and professional elites or attempt to depose them? Will professors align themselves with their boards of trustees or their students? No one knows the answer to such questions, since even such supposedly hard-core conservative groups as big business and the military are riven by internal dissension and debate. It is entirely incorrect to assume, however, as many analysts do, that increasing political turbulence will inevitably push "doubtful" groups to the Right. In the turbulent, disorderly 1850's, the northern business community found its way into the arms of abolitionists and Free-Soilers, just as American farmers moved in the turbulent, disorderly 1930's from a brief flirtation with protofascism into alliance with organized labor and urban immigrant groups. There was, of course, nothing inevitable about these developments. Indeed, what they demonstrate is the *noninevitability* of specific political realignments, and the critical importance, therefore, of continuing ideological competition, political agitation and organization during revolutionary periods. At such times, radical change *is* possible. Therefore, the most foolish thing that either Left, Right or Center could do in the present crisis would be to remain passive out of fear that action might strengthen their enemies.

In any event, a nation which calls itself democratic ought not to fear the people. In the panic over a possible resurgence of the Right one hears echoes of the Federalists' disdain for "the mob," the assumption being that if the masses *really* ruled America, they would (being brutes) brutalize it. (This aristocratic attitude is never too far from the surface of American liberalism.) Once again, however, we see how the establishment protects itself by attacking extremism rather than the causes of extremism. If American working-men, for example, are beginning to act in a dangerously racist fashion, this is not because they are *canaille* but because the present economic and political system has failed them as it has failed the blacks — because they feel compelled to defend the little they have against threatening forces, real or fancied. The democratic response, I should think, is not to manipulate the system so as to deprive "racists" of power, but to meet the challenge squarely in the political arena by persuading workers that their enemies are those who profit from struggle between the poor and the recently poor. Those that will not make such a fight lack faith in the people and in the democratic process. Fortunately for the nation, however, they no longer speak for the young.

The turmoil of the 1960's may well herald the beginning of another revolutionary phase in American history. Sooner or later — and probably sooner — the inability of the present ruling coalition to satisfy the human needs and political demands of its subjects will become clearly apparent, and the processes of political disintegration and reconstruction will accelerate. Hopefully, as the necessity for systemic change is accepted, political violence will be reduced even as political controversy intensifies. For those willing to accept the new age on its own terms, it will be an exhilarating time to be alive.

The "Vi

etween the completion of the first and final drafts of this book, Dr. Martin Luther King, Jr., and Senator Robert F. Kennedy were assassinated; major outbreaks of ghetto violence engulfed Washington, D.C., Chicago, Pittsburgh and Baltimore; students clashed with police at Columbia, San Francisco State, Harvard, and dozens of other universities and colleges; the Democratic national convention in Chicago became a battlefield; and numerous instances of terrorism by and against police occurred throughout the nation. Violence was analyzed on television, from the pulpit and in political platforms, with diverse speakers sounding a common theme: "America the Violent." America was said to be a violent nation and Americans a violent people. We had sinned, we were told, by watching TV westerns and reading perverse books, by condoning unruly demonstrations and mollycoddling lawbreakers. All of which, of course, must stop. No

ent People" Myth

more guns! No more suspended sentences! Shoot to kill!

These slogans and pronouncements evoked a strong feeling of *déjà vu:* Americans had been there before. The self-denunciations and confessions of responsibility, the threats against "lawless elements" and the promises of reform — all seemed discouragingly familiar. In fact, this new version of an old philosophy brings our study full circle. In Chapter 1 we described how advocates of the myth of peaceful progress sought to deprive group violence of its political and social significance by asserting that outbreaks of revolt were un-American, unnecessary, unrepresentative and counterproductive. Clearly, the "violent people" line is merely the same myth warmed over, for it locates the source of all violence in individual souls rather than in the way the political system works.

If anything, however, the new philosophy is an even more dangerous version of the myth than the original. It

189

begins by imposing upon all Americans an unbearable burden of personal responsibility for *all* violence, and ends by relieving most of us — and our system — of any responsibility for *political* violence. Starting as an end product of original sin, violence quickly becomes the responsibility of a very few specific sinners. How often did the Puritan preacher's sermon on the decline of morality end with an exhortation to destroy the pagans! Modern national self-denunciation ends with a new resolve to root out and exterminate the "violent men."

In an intellectual shell game, you must follow the barker's subtle movements with care. When some national figure, a President, churchman or union leader, says that "we" are a violent people, he does not mean that we, the majority, are assassins or rebels, but that we have permitted criminality, assassination and revolt to flourish. Therefore, when he talks about "violent men," he does not refer to decent, respectable, middle-class white folk, but to the unruly, obstreperous mob of criminals, students, juvenile delinquents, Negroes, poor people and psychopaths who are now lumped together as lacking respect for law and order. Those automatically excluded from this category include government officials, policemen and generals. The attack on lawlessness terminologically frees more powerful social groups from responsibility for violence.

In common parlance, "crime rate," for example, refers to black rapists and stickup artists, not white men in ties overstating deductions on their income tax returns or letting slum buildings fall to pieces. "Violence" means stealing a car or getting into a fight, not shooting suspects or bombing Vietnamese villages. "Gun control" translates into taking weapons out of the hands of ghetto residents, not compelling the police to give up their armored cars and flamethrowers. "Conspiracy" means plotting to evade the

draft laws, not manufacturing an incident to involve the
nation in war. As we have suggested, such linguistic and
conceptual distortions inevitably occur when one considers
violence to be unrelated to the political, economic and social systems which, in fact, generate it. By lumping together ghetto riots and television shoot-'em-ups, acts of
draft resistance and acts of reckless driving, one deprives
that violence which *is* political of its political content, so
that it may be treated as sin or as crime, and suppressed.

As our history shows, however, such blindness is dangerous. By so reacting, one risks escalating group violence
to the level of open insurgency and official violence to that
of genocide.

The recrudescence of the "violent people" philosophy is
a sign that we have learned very little in this violent
decade. Daily, as fresh outbreaks continue and new groups
are involved in revolt, the temptation grows to seek scape-
goats and panaceas, to punish and reward, to cut the Gor-
dian knot by some quick and decisive action. Already, impatient voices announce discovery of "the solution" to the
problems of ghetto violence and student revolt: "Shoot to
kill" or "Give private industry a chance," "Arrest all lawbreakers" or "A student on every committee." While the
preachers preach, however, real problems go unsolved and
real questions unanswered. How, in a centralized and in-
terdependent nation, can oppressed communities become
free and powerful? How can every American group and
every citizen be liberated from the deadly burden of increasing dependence on those whom time and fortune have
placed in positions of authority?

Perhaps, through continuing intellectual and political
struggle, answers will begin to emerge in the decade to
come. Wounded by riots, America may begin to understand how the richest and most powerful society in the

191

world can produce so many poor and powerless communities. Bereaved by assassinations, she may uncover a connection between the politics of the Center and the proliferation of groups on the "lunatic fringe." Worried and angry about the young, she may discover in the fight for a less arrogant, more human society her own salvation. A nation armed with such understanding might then do battle against all violence — not just the violence of the forsaken, but that which inheres in great power illegitimately used.

Notes

1. THE MYTH OF PEACEFUL PROGRESS

1. Clifford Geertz, in "Is America by Nature a Violent Society?" *New York Times Magazine*, April 28, 1968, p. 25.
2. Louis Hartz, *The Liberal Tradition in America*, 1955, p. 58.
3. *Report of the National Advisory Commission on Civil Disorders* (Kerner Report), 1968, Bantam edition, pp. 201–202. See also Fred C. Shapiro and James W. Sullivan, *Race Riots New York, 1964*, 1964; Lenora E. Berson, *Case Study of a Riot: The Philadelphia Story*, 1966; University of California at Los Angeles, Institute of Government and Public Affairs, *Los Angeles Riot Study*, 1967; Robert Conot, *Rivers of Blood, Years of Darkness: The Unforgettable Classic Account of the Watts Riot*, 1967; Thomas Hayden, *Rebellion in Newark: Official Violence and Ghetto Response*, 1967; Ronald Goldfarb, *Report on the Washington Riot*, 1969.
4. Kerner Report (see note 3), pp. 128–135. See also P. Meyer, "A Survey of Attitudes of Detroit Negroes after the Riots of 1967," The Urban League of Detroit, 1967; William McCord and John Howard, "Negro Opinions in Three Riot Cities," *American Behavioral Scientist*, March-April 1968; T. M. Tomlinson and David Sears, "Negro Attitudes Toward the Riots," *Los Angeles Riot Study*, 1967 (see note 3); Nathan

Caplan, "The New Ghetto Man: A Review of Recent Empirical Studies," scheduled to appear in the *Journal of Social Issues*, 1969; Jay Schulman, "Ghetto Residence, Political Alienation and Riot Orientation," in *Urban Disorders, Violence and Urban Victimization*, L. Masotti, ed., 1968; Jerome H. Skolnick, *The Politics of Protest*, 1969, Ballantine ed., pp. 145–148.

5. Philip Taft and Philip Ross, "American Labor Violence," in Hugh Davies Graham and Theodore R. Gurr, eds., *Violence in America*, 1969, Bantam ed., p. 281.

6. Daniel Bell, *The End of Ideology*, 1960, rev. ed., 1962, pp. 127 *et seq.*

7. Quoted in Orville J. Victor, *History of American Conspiracies*, 1863, p. 426.

2. MAJOR REVOLTS IN AMERICAN HISTORY

1. The principal historical works from which these descriptions are drawn are listed in the bibliography following the Notes.

2. Jesse T. Carpenter, *The South As a Conscious Minority*, 1930.

3. INDEPENDENCE AND INTERNAL COLONIZATION

1. Samuel Eliot Morison, *Oxford History of the American People*, 1965, p. 570.

4. QUASI-INDEPENDENCE AND LOCAL POWER

1. Richard Hofstadter, *The American Political Tradition*, 1948, pp. 187–188.

2. Morris Janowitz, *Social Control of Escalated Riots*, 1968, pp. 9–10.

3. *Ibid.*, p. 10.

4. See ch. 1, note 5.

5. Mark Twain and Charles Dudley Warner, *The Gilded Age*, 1873.

6. Richard Hofstadter, *The American Political Tradition*, p. 336.

7. Samuel Lubell, *The Future of American Politics*, 1950.

5. RESPONDING TO GROUP VIOLENCE: COUNTERFORCE, REFORM AND TRANSFORMATION

1. Ethan Allen to Governor Thomas Tryon, quoted in Lamar Middleton, *Revolt U.S.A.*, 1938, p. 141.
2. Edward W. Gude, "Understanding Political Violence," Adlai Stevenson Institute Collection, 1968.

6: THE GHETTO REVOLT: A CRISIS OF COLONIALISM

1. *Report of the National Advisory Commission on Civil Disorders* (Kerner Report), Bantam edition, p. 21.
2. Christopher Lasch, *The Agony of the American Left*, 1969, p. 126.
3. Robert Conot, *Rivers of Blood, Years of Darkness*, 1967, p. 465.
4. See, for example, Grier and Cobbs, *Black Rage*, 1968.
5. See, for example, *Six-City Study: A Survey of Racial Attitudes in Six Northern Cities*, Lemberg Center for the Study of Violence, 1967; Nathan Caplan, "The New Ghetto Man" (see ch. 1 note 4).
6. Charles V. Hamilton, in *Urban Violence*, Charles U. Daley, ed., University of Chicago Center for Policy Study, 1969.
7. Robert W. Tucker, *The Just War*, 1960, p. 12.
8. *Ibid.*, p. 60.
9. David Riesman, in "Is America by Nature a Violent Society?" *New York Times Magazine*, April 28, 1968, p. 114.

7. CENTRALISM VS. DECENTRALISM: THE DEEPENING DEBATE

1. James Q. Wilson, *Varieties of Police Behavior*, 1968.
2. California Governor's Commission on the Los Angeles Riots, *Violence in the City — An End or a Beginning?* (McCone Report), 1965.
3. See Robert M. Fogelson, "White on Black: A Critique of the McCone Commission Report on the Los Angeles Riots," *Political Science Quarterly*, September 1967; Bayard Rustin, "The Watts Manifesto and the McCone Report," *Commentary*, March 1966; Robert Blauner, "Whitewash Over Watts,"

Transaction, March-April 1966; Stanley Lieberson and Arnold Silverman, "The Precipitants and Underlying Conditions of Race Riots," *American Sociological Review,* December 1965.

4. *Report of the National Advisory Commission on Civil Disorders* (Kerner Report), pp. 128–135.

5. See works cited in ch. 1 note 4.

6. Daniel P. Moynihan, *Maximum Feasible Misunderstanding: Community Action in the War on Poverty,* 1969.

7. Wilson, *op. cit.* (see note 1).

8. *Ibid.,* p. 297.

9. *Ibid.,* p. 290.

8. *REVOLUTION IN AMERICA*

1. Barrington Moore, *The Social Origins of Dictatorship and Democracy,* 1966; see also "Revolution in America?" in *New York Review of Books,* January 30, 1969.

2. J. Franklin Jameson, *The American Revolution Considered As a Social Movement,* 1940.

3. Charles A. Beard, *An Economic Interpretation of the Constitution,* 1913, 1935.

4. Hannah Arendt, *On Revolution,* 1963.

5. Richard Hofstadter, *The Paranoid Style in American Politics,* 1966, p. xii.

6. Milton Viorst, *Fall From Grace,* 1968, p. 82.

7. John McDermott, "Technology: The Opiate of the Intellectuals," in *New York Review of Books,* July 31, 1969.

Selected Bibliography

GENERAL WORKS ON VIOLENCE AND SOCIAL CHANGE

Arendt, Hannah. *On Revolution.* New York: Viking, 1963.

Bienen, Henry. *Violence and Social Change.* Chicago: University of Chicago Press, 1968.

Brinton, Clarence Crane. *The Anatomy of Revolution.* New York: Norton, 1938.

Coser, Lewis. *The Functions of Social Conflict.* New York: The Free Press, 1956.

Daniels, David H. et al., eds. *Violence and the Struggle for Existence.* Boston: Little, Brown, 1969.

Eckstein, Harry, ed. *Internal War: Basic Problems and Approaches.* New York: The Free Press, 1964.

Friedrich, Carl J., ed. *Revolution.* New York: Atherton, 1966.

Gurr, Theodore A. *The Conditions of Civil Violence.* Princeton, N. J.: Princeton University Press, 1969.

Hobsbawm, Eric J. *Primitive Rebels.* Manchester, England: Manchester University Press, 1959.

Johnson, Chalmers. *Revolutionary Change.* Boston: Little, Brown, 1966.

Lipset, Seymour. *Revolution and Counterrevolution: Change and Persistence in Social Structures.* New York: Basic Books, 1968.

197

Nieburg, H. L. *Political Violence: The Behavioral Process.* New York: St. Martins, 1969.
Wolfgang, Marvin E., ed. *Patterns of Violence.* Vol. 34, *Annals of the American Academy of Political and Social Science,* 1966.

GENERAL WORKS OR SURVEYS ON VIOLENCE IN AMERICA

Graham, H. D., and T. R. Gurr, eds. *Violence in America: Historical and Comparative Perspectives.* New York: Bantam, 1969.
Heaps, Willard A. *Riots, USA, 1765–1965.* New York: Seabury, 1966.
Middleton, Lamar. *Revolt USA.* Harrisburg, Pa.: Stackpole, 1938.
Morison, Samuel Eliot. *The Oxford History of the American People.* New York: Oxford University Press, 1965.
Rich, Bennett Milton. *The Presidents and Civil Disorder.* Washington, D. C.: Brookings Institution, 1941.
Rubenstein, Richard E., and Robert M. Forgelson, eds. *Legacy of Conflict* (44 reprinted volumes). New York: New York Times–Arno Press, 1969.
Skolnick, Jerome H., ed. *The Politics of Protest.* New York: Ballantine, 1969.
Victor, Orville J. *History of American Conspiracies.* New York: J. D. Torrey, 1863.
Wilson, Frederick T. *Federal Aid in Domestic Disturbances, 1787–1903.* Washington, D.C., 1903.

CONFLICT BETWEEN INDIANS AND WHITES

Barrows, William. *The Indian's Side of the Indian Question.* New York: D. Lothrop, 1887.
Foreman, Grant. *Indian Removal.* Norman, Okla.: University of Oklahoma Press, 1932.
Hagan, William T. *American Indians.* Chicago: Chicago University Press, 1961.
Jackson, Helen Hunt. *A Century of Dishonor.* Boston: Little, Brown, 1903.
Macleod, William Christie. *The American Indian Frontier.* London: Kegan Paul, Trench, Trubner, 1928.
Pearce, Roy Harvey. *The Savages of America.* Baltimore: Johns Hopkins Press, rev. ed. 1965.
Tebbel, John. *The Compact History of the Indian Wars.* New York: Hawthorn, 1966.

COLONIAL VIOLENCE

Andrews, Charles M., ed. *Narratives of the Insurrection, 1675–1690*. New York: Scribner's, 1915.

Bellamy, Edward. *The Duke of Stockbridge: A Romance of Shays' Rebellion*. Morristown, N.J.: Silver Burdett, 1900.

Breckenridge, Henry Marie. *History of the Western Insurrection in Western Pennsylvania, Commonly Called the Whiskey Insurrection, 1794*. Pittsburgh: W. S. Haven, 1859.

Brown, Richard Maxwell. *The South Carolina Regulators*. Cambridge, Mass.: Harvard University Press, 1963.

David, W. W. H. *The Fries Rebellion, 1798–1799*. Doylestown, Pa.: Doylestown Publishing Company, 1899.

Starkey, Marion L. *A Little Rebellion*. New York: Knopf, 1955.

Washburn, Wilcomb E. *The Governor and the Rebel: A History of Bacon's Rebellion in Virginia*. Chapel Hill, N.C.: University of North Carolina Press, 1957.

CIVIL WAR AND RECONSTRUCTION VIOLENCE

Aptheker, Herbert. *American Negro Slave Revolts*. Rev. ed. New York: International Publishers, 1969.

Carroll, Joseph C. *Slave Insurrections in the United States, 1800–1865*. New York: Russell & Russell, 1938.

Carpenter, Jesse T. *The South As a Conscious Minority, 1789–1861: A Study in Political Thought*. New York: New York University Press, 1930.

Cash, W. J. *The Mind of the South*. New York: Knopf, 1941.

Filler, Louis. *The Crusade Against Slavery, 1830–1860*. New York: Harper & Row, 1960.

Franklin, John Hope. *Reconstruction After the Civil War*. Chicago: University of Chicago Press, 1961.

Horn, Stanley F. *Invisible Empire: The Story of the Ku Klux Klan, 1866–1871*. Boston: Houghton Mifflin, 1939.

Stampp, Kenneth M. *The Era of Reconstruction, 1865–1877*. New York: Knopf, 1965.

United States Government, House of Representatives. *Report on the Invasion at Harpers Ferry* (36th Congress, 1st session, report no. 278, 1860); *Report of the Joint Select Committee to Inquire into the Condition of Affairs in the Late Insurrectionary States* (report on the Ku Klux Klan, 42nd Congress, 2nd session, report no. 22, 1872); *The Ku Klux Klan* (House Committee on Rules Hearings, 67th Congress, 1st session, 1921). Washington, D.C.: Government Printing Office.

LABOR-MANAGEMENT VIOLENCE

Adamic, Louis. *Dynamite: The Story of Class Violence in America.* pub. 1937; rev. ed. Gloucester, Mass.: Peter Smith, 1963.

Adams, Graham, Jr. *Age of Industrial Violence, 1910–1915.* (The activities and findings of the United States Commission on Industrial Relations.) New York: Columbia University Press, 1966.

Broehl, Wayne G., Jr. *The Molly Maguires.* Cambridge, Mass.: Harvard University Press, 1964.

Bruce, Robert V. *1877: Year of Violence.* Indianapolis, Ind.: Bobbs-Merrill, 1959.

Haywood, William D. *Bill Haywood's Book: The Autobiography of William D. Haywood.* New York: International Publishers, 1929.

Hoxie, Robert Franklin. *Trade Unionism in the United States.* New York: Russell & Russell, 1966.

Hunter, Robert J. *Violence and the Labor Movement.* New York: Macmillan, 1914.

Perlman, Selig. *A History of Trade Unionism in the United States.* New York: Macmillan, 1923.

United States Strike Commission Report on the Chicago Strike of June-July 1894. Washington, D.C.: Government Printing Office, 1895.

Yellen, Samuel. *American Labor Struggles.* New York: S. A. Russell, 1936, reprinted 1956.

NATIVISM, VIGILANTISM AND LYNCH LAW

Bancroft, Hubert H. *Popular Tribunals.* Vol. 2, 1887, reprinted New York: McGraw-Hill, 1967.

Caughey, John W., ed. *Their Majesties the Mob.* Chicago: Chicago University Press, 1960.

Chalmers, David M. *Hooded Americanism.* Gainesville, Fla.: University of Florida Press, 1968.

Cutler, James E. *Lynch Law.* New York: Longmans Green, 1905.

Higham, John. *Strangers in the Land: Patterns of American Nativism 1860–1925.* New Brunswick, N.J.: Rutgers University Press, 1955.

Hofstadter, Richard. *The Paranoid Style in American Politics.* New York: Knopf, 1966.

Raper, Arthur F. *The Tragedy of Lynching.* Chapel Hill, N.C.: University of North Carolina Press, 1933.

URBAN RIOTS AND RACIAL DISORDER

Berson, Lenora E. *Case Study of a Riot: The Philadelphia Story.* New York: Institute of Human Relations Press, 1966.

California Governor's Commission on the Los Angeles Riots. *Violence in the City — An End or a Beginning?* Los Angeles: Jeffries Banknote Co., 1965.

Chicago Commission on Race Relations. *The Negro in Chicago: A Study of Race Relations and a Race Riot.* Chicago: University of Chicago Press, 1922.

Connery, Robert H., ed. *Urban Riots: Violence and Social Change.* New York: Columbia University Academy of Political Science, 1968.

Conot, Robert. *Rivers of Blood, Years of Darkness: The Unforgettable Classic Account of the Watts Riot.* New York: Bantam, 1967.

Daley, Charles U., ed. *Urban Violence.* Chicago: University of Chicago Center for Policy Study, 1969.

Goldfarb, Ronald. *Report on the Washington Riot.* Privately printed, 1969.

Hayden, Thomas, *Rebellion in Newark: Official Violence and Ghetto Response.* New York: Vintage, 1967.

Headley, J. T. *The Great Riots of New York: 1712–1873.* New York: E. B. Treat, 1873.

McCague, James. *The Second Rebellion: The Story of the New York City Draft Riots of 1863.* New York: Dial, 1968.

Report of the National Advisory Commission on Civil Disorders (Kerner Report). New York: Bantam, 1968.

Shapiro, Fred C. and James W. Sullivan. *Race Riots New York 1964.* New York: Crowell, 1964.

University of California at Los Angeles. *Los Angeles Riot Study.* Los Angeles: Institute of Government and Public Affairs, 1967.

Waskow, Arthur I. *From Race Riot to Sit-In.* Garden City, N.Y.: Doubleday, 1966.